Bill Borcherdt, ACSW, BCD

Fundamentals
of Cognitive-Behavior Therapy:
From Both Sides of the Desk

D0146947

Pre-publication
REVIEWS,
COMMENTARIES,
EVALUATIONS . . .

"**T**herapists who practice Rational Emotive Behavior Therapy (REBT) and related forms of Cognitive-Behavior Therapy (CBT) can use a number of important questions to probe their clients' dysfunctional beliefs and behaviors and encourage them to think more rationally and wisely for themselves. Bill Borcherdt, in this unusually clear and practical book, includes a wide selection of these trenchant questions. He also gives a great many sensible and therapeutic answers to common questions that clients, to their own detriment, ask their therapists. Both beginning and experienced practitioners of REBT, CBT, and other cognitive-oriented therapies will find a considerable number of valuable suggestions in Bill Borcherdt's book."

Albert Ellis, PhD
President,
Institute for Rational-Emotive
Therapy, New York City;
Author, *Better, Deeper and More
Enduring Brief Therapy*

More pre-publication
REVIEWS, COMMENTARIES, EVALUATIONS . . .

"**F**or many years, I have recommended Borcherdt's other books to Rational Recovery Self-Help Network (RRSN) participants. With this book, he has surpassed himself and produced a handbook that will instruct and inspire any reader who will open it to any page. Borcherdt's *Fundamentals of Cognitive-Behavior Therapy* is an absolutely fascinating presentation of the very best concepts of general self-help in a highly readable dialog format. When I had read only a few pages, I felt I was sitting in the arena with Socrates, learning through bullet-nosed questions that get at the answers. But the material covered is right on target, with solutions for today's problems. Anyone with a substance abuse problem can look forward to tackling the aftermath of addiction by reading this book. I heartily recommend it to anyone interested in personal growth and self-improvement."

Jack Trimpey, LCSW
Founder, President,
Rational Recovery Systems, Inc.

"**I**f you aren't familiar with Bill Borcherdt's writings, you're in for a treat. He is precise, informed, and always original. To make the subject of mental health intriguing is not easy. However, Bill Borcherdt manages it quite well if his readers will but give him their attention.

I can assure you this work is complete, detailed, and penetrating. His thoughts are so well-organized that when he explains the advantages of asking the client, "What do you think about what I'm saying?" he manages to offer no less than 13 reasons for so doing. To Question Number 28: 'Why don't I change? Why do I keep goofing up?' he offers ten answers. He gives the same thoroughness to the other 171 rational questions, some of which need to be addressed in all counseling sessions for maximum benefit.

This book exemplifies Borcherdt's best gifts: pleasurable reading and original ideas. I know of no other author who has endeavored to expound on something as unique as his '173 rational inquiries . . . for identifying those questions that will increase the chances of prompting helpful goal-directed responses from clients.'

The Haworth Press, Inc.

Fundamentals
of Cognitive-Behavior
Therapy
From Both Sides of the Desk

HAWORTH Social Work Practice
Carlton E. Munson, DSW, Senior Editor

New, Recent, and Forthcoming Titles:

Fundamentals
of Cognitive-Behavior
Therapy
From Both Sides of the Desk

Bill Borcherdt, ACSW, BCD

The Haworth Press
New York • London

The Haworth Press, Inc., 10 Alice Street, Binghamton, NY 13904-1580

Borcherdt, Bill.
   Fundamentals of cognitive-behavior therapy : from both sides of the desk / Bill Borcherdt.
      p.   cm.
   Includes index.
   ISBN 0-7890-6030-2 (hardcover : alk. paper)
   1. Cognitive therapy. 2. Interviewing in psychiatry. 3. Psychotherapist and patient. I. Title.
RC489.C63B67 1996
616.89′142–dc20   96-5122
                                                                                                  CIP

To all of my past and present associates at Clinical Services of Winnebago County in Wisconsin, the best mental health clinic in existence. With admiration for your mounds of professional wisdom and with fond appreciation for your abundant contributions of the past 26 years that have made it more convenient for me to come more into my own as a provider of mental health services, and more important, as a human being.

ABOUT THE AUTHOR

Bill Borcherdt, ACSW, BCD, is a psychotherapist at Clinical Services of Winnebago County in Neenah, Wisconsin, and is also in private practice in Menasha, Wisconsin. He has 28 years of clinical experience in mental health clinics and 23 years of private practice counseling with individuals, couples, parents, families, and groups who have varying degrees of emotional and relationship problems. He frequently teaches graduate, undergraduate, and continuing education courses for the University of Wisconsin System, and has served as an adjunct faculty member at four colleges and universities. Mr. Borcherdt has over 400 state and national workshop programs to his credit and is well known for his interesting and witty presentations that have practical application to everyday professional and personal life. His first two books, *Think Straight! Feel Great!* and *You Can Control Your Feelings!* were chosen by Behavioral Science Book Service as featured selections. His forthcoming book is entitled *The Joys of Rational Loving.*

CONTENTS

SECTION I.
ASKING RATIONAL QUESTIONS AND GETTING THERAPEUTIC ANSWERS: A COGNITIVE-BEHAVIOR INTERVIEWING GUIDE

Introduction

This section of 173 rational inquiries is a nuts-and-bolts, "hands-on" listing designed as a convenient reference source for identifying questions that will increase the chances of prompting helpful goal-directed responses from clients. A central premise of cognitive-behavior therapy is that individuals bring themselves to their emotions and behaviors by how they think. Each question posed in this section examines some of the thoughts, feelings, and behaviors it is intended to prompt. Each in its own way has the potential for the client to piggyback off into thoughts, feelings, and behaviors that would be more in his/her best interest, thus helping to pave the way toward more long-range happiness. Clients seldom conform to the ideal and rather than mark time in the problem-solving interview process, one of these questions can be interjected to keep the problem-solving focus moving along. Therapeutic efficiency can be maintained by extending the problem-solving intent in calling upon rational questions. The goal of each inquiry is to get at the jugular vein of clients' emotional disturbances quicker and to more readily and thoroughly assist the client in correcting these upsets. Ideally, in time clients will be able to become their own best therapists by confronting themselves with these very questions that the counselor has used to help them to help themselves. The only distinction would be that clients would substitute "I," "my," or "me" for "you" or "your" in their self-questioning confrontations, e.g., "How will I handle the problem situation the next time it comes up?" "How do I keep myself from achieving my goals?" "What would be a good homework assignment for me to work on my problem?" By answering their own questions individuals can expose their own solutions.

Whether it be the student in training, beginning clinician, or seasoned practitioner, all helpers often ask themselves questions about what to say next at various problem-solving points of entry.

The student may ask him/herself, "When a client comes for help, what do I say and do?" The beginning clinician wading into the reality that clients seldom conform to the textbook ideal may self-inquire, "I never realized that it could be so different face-to-face with clients rather than reading about clients–now what do I say and how do I carry myself in this uncharted situation?" Even the veteran of many problem-solving interviewing wars will often ask, "This problem is different in its own way from any others that I have previously dealt with–what would be a good question that might expose grist for the therapeutic mill?"

This listing of therapeutic questions is not an exhaustive one. It is hoped that it will both supplement those interventive inquiries you already use as well as make it convenient for you to branch off to create new ones of your own. As you review each one you may find yourself triggering independent questioning ideas to add further to your line-of-questioning repertoire. I think good grass-roots problem-solving questions are not only difficult to find but are also commodities that are difficult to run out of. All can serve as general problem-solving questions for whatever problem-solving treatment modality is used, but are especially included with those who practice some form of cognitive-behavior therapy in mind. What is now called Rational Emotive Behavior Therapy (REBT) was invented by Albert Ellis, PhD, in 1955. It is a specialized form of cognitive-behavior therapy; many of the questions in this listing stem from my training in REBT at the Institute for Rational Emotive Behavior Therapy in New York City. Those interested in getting the institute's catalog of books, many other therapeutic resources, and professional training programs can write to: Institute for Rational-Emotive Therapy, 45 East 65th Street, New York, New York 10021.

One of the main goals in helping clients to help themselves get past their hesitations, avoidances, overreactions, and personalizations is to set the stage for them to provide therapeutic answers to our questions. Therapeutic questions are those that make it more convenient for the client to think, feel, and act in ways that would likely contribute more to their long-range happiness and survival. What some of these direct, straightforward, rational questions are is the subject of this text. "Give a man a fish and he will eat for today; teach him how to fish and he will eat for a lifetime." All of the following client-directed "you" questions encourage the consumer to think for him/herself so as to encourage the type of independent thinking that will generate ideas to better cope not only with the presenting problem, but with practically any problem under the sun in the future. Telling clients what to do may help them cope for today; encouraging self-reliant thinking, a skill that can be applied today and in the future, will assist in coping for a lifetime.

"You" Questions:
Rational Inquiries That Active-Directively Seek Out the Client's View

What follows is an abundance of "you" questions that not only can effectively lead to developing plans on how to make things right but can, more comprehensively, show how to efficiently get oneself less upset when things go wrong. Not that "you" questions are the "only" way to go by way of leading interventive questioning, but they are preferable because they get the client directly involved in correcting self-created faulty thoughts, feelings, and behaviors. At times it is better to "tell" clients what the reality of the situation is as you and/or others see it. When clients are heavily distorting, denying, or overlooking or are drifting and meandering around for other reasons, we can do them a favor by honestly zeroing in on identifying their resistances as we see them. But even here, when we lead with an "I" statement we can often combine it with a "you" question, thus redirecting the client back to self-responsibility for framing and formulating his or her own perspectives, e.g., "I think you've worked hard at convincing yourself that you 'can't' do it, which to me explains why you're hardly working—what do *you* think about what I'm saying?"

ADVANTAGES OF "YOU" QUESTIONS

Some advantages of "you" questions that seek out client views include:

1. "You" questions are difficult to refute. Asking others' opinion about a topic is a form of flattery and there are only two types of people who enjoy such adulation: men and women. The

communication behind the "you" asking is, "what you say is important or I wouldn't bother to inquire." It is more difficult for a client to resist desired teachings when his or her input into what is being taught is assertively sought. Four little words, "what do you think," conveniences the client's gravitating more toward ideas presented.

2. "You" questions get the client more involved. Learning is not a spectator sport. Involvement lubricates learning. Cognitive-behavior therapies wish to teach clients new ways of looking at, feeling about, and behaving toward old problems. One of the best ways to facilitate such learning is to meet clients on their own turf by striving to rattle the cages of their opinions. A Chinese proverb states, "Tell me and I'll forget, show me and I may remember, involve me and I'll understand." Understanding the clients' understanding by prompting them to get their opinions out on the table encourages active, direct-involvement problem-solving.

3. "You" questions are a vote of confidence. By asking clients what would be a different, better way to think, feel, or act about their problems, you are acknowledging their ability to think and to problem-solve for themselves; that they are not emotional cripples who need someone to direct their life.

4. "You" questions encourage client-therapist collaboration. Inviting opinion is inviting the clients to go from the opposite side of the table, "fighting" the therapist, to the same side of the table to fight the problem.

5. "You" questions curtail client resistances. When the stage is set for the client to respond to his own ideas he will be less likely to resist doing better. Getting the client to follow his own nose lessens the chances of his sticking up his nose at advice presented.

6. "You" questions promote individual responsibility. They encourage the development of a client's own problem-solving agenda and convey a personal accountability for finding such remedies.

7. "You" questions prompt an awareness of the problem along with a glimmer of new ideas that would more expose potential solutions.

8. "You" questions pave the way for specific recommendations for change, including cognitive, emotive, and behavioral homework assignments that directly attack the problem.

9. "You" questions begin to acknowledge the repeated discipline and hard work practically always required to achieve a better result. Fine-tuned questions encourage disciplined thinking, setting the stage for more well-practiced behavior.

10. "You" questions indirectly attack low frustration tolerance (LFT). Perhaps the primary motivation for resistance to change is LFT, exaggerating the difficulty the client must go through to achieve a given result. "You" questions imply that things can be done, progress can be made, and it's not "too hard" to begin to plan to think, feel, and act in ways that will contribute to a higher level of self-actualization.

11. "You" questions shorten the problem-solving process by illustrating solutions while making it more inconvenient for the client to pretend to not know what is known. As the client is encouraged to respond to therapeutic questions she is more likely to make herself aware of her own problem-solving resources while keeping herself on the track of individual responsibility for creating her own solutions.

12. "You" questions maintain problem-solving intensity by keeping focused on the problem at hand. Rather than once-over-lightly doing a little bit of a lot of things but not much of any one thing, the corrective interviewing process is made more meaningful by establishing problem-solving territory and working within it. Client and therapist are less likely to go off on watered-down conversational tangents with the use of questions that redirect such drifting.

13. "You" questions create expectations of more doing and less stewing. Perhaps the ultimate test of therapeutic effectiveness is whether the client gets off his/her backside and goes after what is wanted while refusing to accept what is not wanted by way of personal ambitions. Each question listed tenders active-directive movement by the client in more adventurously testing out slices of life heretofore not sampled.

SAMPLES OF "YOU" QUESTIONS

Each of the questions posed in this section is followed by commentary relating to the rationale behind the asking and to hoped-for responses, including what new manner of thought, feeling, and behavior it will hopefully and preferably encourage.

1.   "What would life be like without your problem?"
Few people will consider personal change until they realize that there are some definite advantages in the change. Expanding the clients' awareness as to the advantages plants the seeds of commitment to and hope for constructive change. Clients identifying advantages to change can lead into a referenting homework assignment of listing on a notecard all those pluses that would befall them in the aftermath of change. These can then be appreciatively reviewed daily by the client for five to ten minutes per day as a motivation enhancer.

2.   "What is something that would be wise for you to do to work on your problem?"
The action component of the helping process is suggested and can be followed by client-helper collaboration on specific between-sessions activity-behavioral tasks that would provide the client with an opportunity to work directly on his/her problem, e.g., say "no" three times, apply for five jobs, or give three compliments in the next week, to name a few.

3.   "What were you doing differently in your life when you were without the problem?"
It's often easier to build from strengths rather than from weaknesses. Rather than using the past as a reliable source of misery it can be touched upon as a means of accessing capabilities. It's usually easier to do something that one has done before, and identification of past helpful coping mechanisms can rekindle use of these strategies in the present. By asking the client to list what and how he has done right in past, similar problematic life circumstances can inspire hope, realistic optimism, and performance confidence. This makes the client aware

that actions to rectify the presenting problem are nothing that he/she hasn't done before and can provoke enlightened self-interest in tackling the problem.

4. "How could you peacefully coexist with the problem if need be?"
Oftentimes behind every storm cloud there isn't a silver lining; maybe the solution to a problem is to accept that there is no solution. A positive thinker frequently presents as somebody who says, "Cheer up—things are going my way," somebody who thinks he has the world by the ass on a downward pull—and wants you to be happy about it. Successful psychotherapy outcomes are not necessarily those when clients change personality tendencies or realign faulty transactions within their social group, but when they are more willing to accept inevitable imperfections within themselves, within their relationships with important others, or with the world at large. This question begins to alert the client to begin to consider what to realistically expect of imperfect people in an imperfect world. Such undamning acceptance of the inevitable deficiencies that usually don't change (or if they do change, reappear as a different garden variety) goes a long way toward a mentally healthier existence.

Also, this inquiry encourages the client to take pressure off herself by introducing the enlightened idea that she doesn't "have to" get over her practical and/or emotional predicaments and that it is not "awful" if she doesn't. Such increased acceptance and tolerance implies that because some parts of life are deficient it is not necessary to rate an entire existence as miserable. When the client takes pressure off herself for continuing to have problems, she puts herself in a better position to change situations that, to whatever degree, can be changed.

5. "How will you handle the problem situation the next time it arises?"
Pasteur said, "Chance favors the prepared mind." Mark Twain said, "It takes me three months to prepare for an

impromptu speech." A large part of doing psychotherapy is preparing the client for the real world. Prevention is more efficient than cure. In addition to getting the client to organize and mobilize his resources before the heat of battle, this question provides a vote of self-confidence. By asking clients their plan of action rather than telling them one, you profess confidence in their problem-solving skills while implying their responsibility in taking the initiative to use those skills. Homework assignments in prevention might involve rehearsing in the client's imagination the style of his coping method or behaviorally rehearsing with him tact and tactics of better dealing with the person or circumstances of concern. Such methods well practiced in the present can be translated into spontaneity or second-nature responses in the future.

6. "How are you going to contradict your mistaken ideas about the problem in the future?"
   The message here is, "You can think for yourself and part of the expectation of your therapy is that you do just that." This underlying no-nonsense philosophy directs the client toward emotional self-sufficiency providing a glimpse of the advisability of marching to the tune not of a different drummer but of his/her own drummer. Assign homework that will help the client identify and practice prepared coping statements that can be used when accosted by the problem. Better yet, teach the client to stop and think via use of the scientific method. This will likely produce even longer-lasting results because more force and effort is put into scientific disputations, yielding a higher return on a higher energy investment. Suggest to the client that he practice catching mistaken beliefs by self-questions, e.g., "Where is the proof?" "Where is the evidence?" "Where can it be verified?" This helps ensure that the notion under scrutiny is accurate.

7. "Do humans always have to do what is best? Why or why not?"

By introducing the client to a glance at human limitations and fallibility the therapist sets the stage for active forgiveness later on. Much therapy, when done under a rational-living umbrella, promotes self- and other forgiveness as the most important cornerstone. The first push in problem solving is often the hardest. The helping process practically stops until self- and/or other downing is curtailed. The client is alerted to the value of self- and other permissiveness by initiating the right rational question.

8. "What is your present view of your problem?"
   This introductory question can help clients consider that thoughts are important, that humans usually feel the way they think. This query also strikes a chord of hope leading into identifying the specific explanatory, self-sentences that create the emotional upset and what their more helpful replacements might be. A person who is aware of options in thinking can create more desirable emotions. This is a hopeful platform from which to problem-solve.

9. "What are the effects of your present ideas and how do they cause you to feel?"
   This follow-up to number 8 introduces consequential thinking in that the client is asked to evaluate the consequences of his or her present way of thinking.

10. "How could you think differently so as to not make yourself feel upset?"
    Logic and reason in the service of the clients' emotions are pursued in a way that encourages the client to begin to see that he has the capacity to consider his thinking in a more logical, precise way.

11. "Can you use more information on how to make things right or on how to get yourself less upset when things go wrong?"
    Making things right is the tip of the human condition iceberg. Life contains hassles that won't go away, that are too numerous to mention. Positive thinking would be better replaced with tolerant, accepting thinking. This question is a wake-up call for the client since it begins to

alert her to the hopeful reality that adversities in her life don't have to be made right before she can begin to better cope with them. Knowing that negative conditions of life don't have to be controlled before one can manage one's emotions lessens feelings of futility that inevitably occur when trying to regulate outside forces.

12. "Do you think there is a connection between how you think and how you feel? If so, what in your own words is it?"
    Getting clients to acknowledge this basic thought-feeling connection premise and then requesting that they verbalize their understanding to you enables them to begin to more logically organize their understanding of this basic idea. Once this central idea is accepted and described by the client the counselor can therapeutically relate back to it, e.g., by asking, "What did you tell yourself just before you made yourself feel upset?" Getting clients to record-keep their own emotions by identifying during the week unwanted emotions, the thoughts immediately preceding them, and countering rational thoughts that would put a damper on the upset can be advised.

13. "What types of self-instructions have you been giving yourself that account for your unwanted feelings?"
    Clients teach themselves nonsense that in turn creates dysfunctional emotions. Creating their own more flexible, well-thought-out self-instructional booklet originates in this type of question that reviews and disclaims ideas that to date have not best served emotional well-being.

14. "What better meaning can you attach to your difficult situation?"
    Humans have a flair for the insignificant. They make sacred inconveniences while defining themselves by their life circumstances. The therapeutic trick is to invite, if not persuade, clients to overreact less and accept themselves more. This is a simple/not easy task, but it would be advisable to start someplace. This question helps pave the way toward philosophies of anti-awfulizing and anti-

catastrophizing while gaining a sense that as troublesome as life might become, as important as some things are, they still are not all-important.

15. "What would be a good homework assignment that will help you to work on your problem?"
Most therapy takes place *outside* of the office. Knowing and not doing is the same as not knowing. Insight may cure ignorance but it doesn't solve emotional problems. What can accomplish the latter is vigorously acting against one's fears, anxieties, depression, shame, etc.— and the irrational beliefs that cause them. The best way to change an irrational idea is to act against it. If the client procrastinates about pinpointing what he can do to work on his problem the other 167 hours of the week, beyond the nonsacred, nonmagical one-hour-per-week office visit, you may have to suggest some ideas. Or if he assigns himself a task that he is incapable of completing, or one that doesn't address his problem, e.g., a dull normal person assigning himself a technical book to read, a paranoid schizophrenic taking on a direct social assignment, or a person who is thirty pounds overweight planning to lose twenty pounds within two weeks, it may be better for you to do the client a favor by confronting and cutting through such unrealism with direct homework proposals of your own. My main point is—doing gets it done so see to it that the client has some activity to do, other than therapy homework assignments. In that self-discovery is preferable, such homework possibilities should be generated by the client—but not necessarily so.

16. "How can you more strongly believe what you know to be true and helpful?"
Use of force in problem solving sometimes seems like a lost art. When people disturb themselves they very forcefully convince themselves to believe inaccurate, disturbance-producing ideas. To unconvince and undisturb themselves will likely require a strong emotive countering of the up-until-now exaggerated, personalized train

of thought. The client who makes a tape recording of herself remedying false ideas by challenging their validity uses one technique that responds to the value of vigorously countering ideas that cause emotional disruption. This question lets the client know the often overlooked advantages of not only telling oneself rational ideas, but talking to oneself about them—preferably in staunch, profound, hard-hitting ways.

17. "How can you better convince yourself to increase the effort to do what is in your long-run best interest?"
This companion question of number 16 pushes for examination of self-motivation for going beyond the cognitive to the behavioral component of change. Inner growth should include outer movement. Introducing an "as if" philosophy of problem solving can help in putting forth the behavioral effort required to achieve a given result. Impressing upon the client the value of getting him/herself to the task whether feeling like it or not, is the long and short of self-propelling "as if" behavior.

18. "How can you commit yourself to the idea that it is not what you know that is so important, but what you do with what you know?"
Putting a bug in clients' ears that knowledge is pale compared to action readies them to avoid a once-over-lightly approach to more helpful activity. The message of this question is "Ask not what your therapy can do for you, but ask what you can do for your therapy." If clients are going to be helped, they are going to actively work for their therapy rather than expect it to work for them. The more your line of questioning ties into the idea that matters of life and psychotherapy are not accomplished in the dugout, the better.

19. "How do your present ways of thinking make it more difficult for you to navigate life?"
Leading clients to turn on their own therapeutic guiding cognitive light can be done by first getting them to "fess

up" to those dysfunctional thoughts that stand in the way of avoiding blind alleys en route to finding their way home.

20. "Do events upset you, or do you upset yourself about events?"

    To begin to examine the idea that humans affect themselves more than they are affected is a giant step toward more humanistic problem solving in that it puts the individual in the driver's seat for better controlling his emotions. Circumstances, systems, and people do not have to change before the individual can begin to help himself carve out a better life-style. When the individual understands that he upsets himself it allows him to jump-start personal change while activating George Bernard Shaw's position regarding self-responsibility: "Things don't happen to me, I happen to them."

21. "When thinking changes, feelings change. What thoughts have you changed to make yourself feel better?"

    Steering clients in the direction of seeing themselves not only as active participants in their own disturbance but also as being a meaningful part of undisturbing themselves permits a well-rounded appraisal of one's own responsibility for one's emotional well-being. This question helps to earmark those "thoughts that work" by way of producing more desirable emotional results.

22. "What do you think would be a better plan?"

    Forging ahead therapeutically can be done by prompting clients to become their own best scientist. This inquiry asks clients to identify their hypothesis and then get a data base to confirm or disconfirm its validity. This simple question encourages clients to think, develop their own road map, test it out, and learn from conclusions drawn from the journey.

23. "What value do you see in change?"

    High on the success measurement of the helping methods used is the ability to get clients to convince you why it is in their best interest to change. Getting them to itemize and to more fully appreciate each item on the "what life would be like if I changed" scale creates incentive for doing things differently and doing different things.

24. "How do you keep yourself from achieving your goals?"
Concluding themselves to be their own worst enemy, minus putting themselves down for self-created road-blocks, redirects clients in a direction of more personal accountability. The more questions that are directed toward leading clients to see that they trip their own emotional triggers, the more responsibility for self and for emotional self-control will likely be generated.

25. "How does your thinking really cause you to feel?"
Inner emotional control, regardless of outer turmoil, can be maintained with scientific, flexible thinking. This question is designed to spark this hopeful, emotionally self-sufficient view. Until the client understands the thinking-feeling connection he/she will likely blame outside factors for emotional upsets.

26. "Do you want to continue to disturb yourself?"
The near-obvious answer to this question is designed to begin to envision alternatives generally, and alternative thinking specifically about those tacts and tactics that have not done justice to personal happiness. After the client responds "no" to the question, the counselor can begin to use that response as a baseline from which to confront the client later in the interview, e.g., when the client proclaims herself upset, she can be brought back to her original statement and be asked to brainstorm ideas on how she can contribute toward her original goal of not upsetting herself. By the client's "no" response the green light to find solutions to the client's problems starts to go on and, until such permission from the client to explore ways to gain more inner harmony is given, the therapeutic show cannot go on.

27. "Because you like things to be a certain way does that mean they should, must, or have to be that way?"
Giving the client a direct hint as to the detrimental effects of his demandingness can begin with this well-timed

question. As the demand is uncovered and agreed upon as being such, it can then be tied into life circumstances that activated it. Discussion about its pernicious side-effects and instructions for deactivating its emotionally contaminating nature can then be carried forth.

28. "If you have the freedom to choose not to like something, do not others also have the right to believe as they choose?" The idea that people have free will and not the client's will is an important concept to provide background information for. Demandingness is at the core of much human disturbance and the beginnings of countering such irrational insistences can be jogged with this question. One of the biggest challenges facing the human condition generally, and psychotherapy specifically, is to meet head on the tendency for individuals to baffle themselves as to how anyone can think differently than they. Until a decent respect for individual difference is established, interpersonal conflict rather than accommodation is likely to dominate. Knifing into the interview with this assertive inquiry reviews and revives this permissive view that when applied, instills emotional slack into individual differences.

29. "If you select and bias yourself against others' values, don't they have the right to opinionize against yours?" Emotional anguish follows clinging to the ultra ideal that others have no right to betray one's sacred values. By reflecting on "what's good for the goose is good for the gander" it can be more easily understood that others in fact do have the right to discriminate against your ideals, just as you have against theirs. Introducing the client to the emotional relief equation "take the sacredness out of your values and you will take much pressure out of your life" can be accomplished by client and counselor examining this interesting question.

30. "Are not others more for themselves than against you?" It is reality that a large majority of people who oppose our beliefs seek to express their values more than they seek to oppose us. This realization can begin to pave the

way toward a less personalized, hypersensitive, defensive life's philosophy. Understanding and accepting that dissenters are not out to get us creates less guarded social relationships in which people can agree to disagree without hurt and anger.

31. "Do others have free choice or your choice?"
Getting clients to dismount from their high horses often requires repeated confrontive questioning. Getting them to see that they don't run the universe (yet) can be forthrightly done by this free-will-type question. Simply getting consumers to acknowledge that others have "free choice, not my choice" can provide marked emotional relief for them. Assigning them the task of practicing this and similar coping statements between sessions often results in increased emotional relief and higher energy levels. To protest against reality saps energy; to accept reality creates energy.

32. "Would you always want to get what you deserve?"
This challenging question begins to punch holes in the theory that (a) there is such an animal as "deservingness" and (b) it is a desirable thing. To get clients to look more broadly at the common demand for equity they must accept that they get what they get and not what they deserve; what they get, not necessarily what they want. Besides, if there were a deservingness guarantee many would be inside the institution looking out! This confronting question takes the steam out of irrational insistences that laws of deservingness bend one's way only when it is to one's advantage that such favoritism exist.

33. "Why must you be the one person in the universe who always gets his own way and who receives never-ending kind and fair treatment?"
Most people operate under the misconception that they are "special" and therefore are automatically entitled to "special" favors and treatment by the world and the people in it. Punching holes in this self-centered view and its "I'm anointed" fallacy can begin to jar clients

into coming to their senses and realizing that they aren't the center of the universe after all. Bursting the grandiose bubble can lead the way to a more humbling but realistic perspective as to one's place in the overall earthly scheme of things.

34. "What advantage is it for you to whine and scream when you don't get your own way?"
The truth sometimes doesn't taste good, but it can strengthen the gut on the way down. Honesty is usually the best policy when interviewing clients. If you believe that emotional disturbance is often self-created by whining and screaming that one isn't getting one's own way, then sooner rather than later it would be helpful to be honest enough to clue your client in to your hypothesis. Then, ask him/her what he/she thinks of that idea and whether he/she is willing to give up such tantrums.

35. "Though you would like life to be fair, does it have to be? Must it be?"
The front page of the newspaper informs us of the obvious, often forgotten reality that life is not fair. A flawed philosophy of fairness underlies much emotional disturbance. Exposing this illusion of fairness and the demand that something exist that does not exist—namely fairness—prods the client in the right direction of accepting life as it is.

36. "Would all people in your circumstance think and feel the way you do about it?"
Identifying alternative ways of looking at the same problem can encourage the client to sample healthier, more helpful perspectives. Free will in choosing alternative methods of thought can be exercised in a way that can allow the client to emotionally rise above his/her problematic circumstance. Supplying common illustrations can help cement this notion of different ways of looking at old problems, e.g.: "If there were one hundred people at a picnic, and the picnic were canceled due to rain, would all one hundred people be upset?" "If fifty people were criticized harshly, would all make themselves feel

angry?" "If there were one hundred people released from a concentration camp, would they all cope the same about their time in captivity?" In each example, it is advisable to seek out with the client what was different about those individuals who didn't overreact to adversity. This could produce higher-level possibilities of thought and feeling.

37. "What advice would you give to a friend who had your problems?"
     Granted, good advice is easier to give than it is to follow—but that doesn't take away from the fact that it is good advice. Humans frequently give themselves a bad case of reverse arrogance, believing that it is understandable and acceptable that others make mistakes and have problems as mere mortals, but that they as noble souls are not allowed such a luxury as fallibility. This perfectionistic double standard can be challenged by getting the client to illustrate to him/herself that encouragement would do well to begin at home. Neither exaggerating the significance of a problem nor putting oneself down for having it is a compassionate view that can be transposed from others to self. Instruct a client to give him/herself for one day the same advice that he/she would give to a friend in a similar tough situation. This helps to illuminate what the client can do for him/herself by way of acceptance of self enroute to better emotional well-being.

38. "Do you get angry or do you make yourself angry?"
     Anger stems from other-blaming. Getting clients to see that they trip their own anger trigger, that the anger enemy is themselves and not the other person, is often done in little doses. This is because clients find it difficult to admit to their own dependent, demanding, intolerant personality deficiencies that cause their anger. Human defensiveness is seen when individuals are reluctant to admit responsibility for their overreactions because they assume if they did they would be required to blame themselves. Pointing a finger at another and emphatically stat-

ing "You make me mad!" relieves the self-blame tendency. This question hopes to get the client to hold him/herself accountable for his/her anger without self-condemnation for having it.

39. "Do you believe in free will or determinism?"
Practically all clients I have posed this question to acknowledge the existence of free will. Yet, when it comes to applying its implication–anything they or someone else believes can be disbelieved–action falls short of belief. When it comes to themselves, clients will communicate "But I've thought and been this way all of my life." When it pertains to others, clients often state, "Who does he think that he is, thinking and acting in ways that I would never even remotely think of." Carved-in-granite expectations of self and up-on-a-high-horse demands of others do not contribute to long-range personal and interpersonal happiness and survival.

40. "Do others really get inside your gut and give you feelings?"
Acknowledging that there is no such thing as an emotional transplant, that no one has ever invented a way to instill a feeling into someone else, is one of the most basic principles of mental health. To recognize this frees one emotionally so that one is not at the mercy of another. Knowing that feelings cannot be given helps to bring down the protective guard so that one can deal more cordially with one's social group.

41. "Were you given beliefs, scripted, or did you invent them, script yourself?"
This sharply contrasted inquiry is worded so that more accountability for one's beliefs can be suggested. Humans are creators of ideas; they are not passively spoon-fed their current philosophies of life, but are active participants in their manufacture. Clients will often say: "Where did I get that idea?" "How did I ever come across that way of thinking?" "Whatever possessed me to start thinking that way?" Believing that there are spe-

cial formulas that determine beliefs can lead to a wild-goose chase in searching for something that doesn't exist. For example, very few children have been told by parent figures that they are "no good" or "will never amount to anything," yet there are millions of people walking this green earth who regularly feel inferior. They almost automatically give themselves feelings of self-deprecation *not* because someone told them they are worthless but because they concocted ideas such as "my faults = my worthlessness" on their own. The goal is to help clients become less talented at creating self-defeating ideas and more skilled at countering such self-imposed, illogical manners of thinking.

42. "Do you magically get inside others' guts and give them feelings?"
Humans tend to flatter themselves. Rather than give themselves a sense of humility as to what they can and can't do to and for others, they immodestly believe that they can hand over a feeling to another. This false idea often leads to feelings of guilt and pity and blocks more assertive, self-interested behavior. It is wiser to understand that although you can inconvenience and frustrate others, they decide whether they are going to push the buttons (called whining and screaming) about the dissatisfactions you created. This can unshackle you toward more informal, enjoyable interactions with others.

43. "Where is the evidence that you have to be perfect?"
Confucius said, "To try to go beyond is as wrong as to fall short." Demanding perfectionism of self, others, and life is the tripod of emotional disturbance and the pursuit of *un*happiness. Getting clients not only to know but to know well the value of directly disputing this impossible command will save much emotional wear and tear. Clients can be taught to interrupt superhuman dictates as soon as they notice their occurrence by self-debating the very premise "Where is it written, where is the evidence that I have to do perfectly well?" Emotional relief is

likely to follow from such a psychological, scientific exploration.

44. "Do you have to damn yourself when you don't do the right thing, and where does such self-blame get you emotionally?"

To err is human, to blame is even more human. One of humans' favorite pastimes is self-downing. Finding emotionally healthier manners of expression can be introduced via this inquiry aimed at abolishing self-flagellation tendencies. Until self-blame is minimized it is unlikely that the client will get out of the problem-solving starting blocks. Encouraging forgiveness of self for having problems and shortcomings should stand in front of attempts to change them and that more energy can be put into correcting these handicaps that would otherwise be lost in berating oneself for having them.

45. "Is there any truth to the idea that others have to treat you fairly because you treat them fairly?"

"Others should do unto me as I do unto them" is the battle cry of those who invent such a "reverse golden rule." Happiness being a direct ratio between what one expects and what one gets leaves unhappiness when the demanding plea for behavioral equity goes unheard. The idea of "one hand washes the other" ("if I take care of your emotional wants from me, then you must do the same for mine") has no objective basis in reality. It is the counselor's responsibility to sooner rather than later introduce this grim but instructional reality to the client. This question can serve as a springboard to do just that.

46. "Why must others not treat you with lapses in kindness and consideration?"

This asking is another attempt to draw out and eventually abolish irrational thinking that presumes fairness and partiality is to ever flow from others. Putting a dent in this idea of eminent justice that others must treat us with no deficiencies in pleasantry reduces the stress and strain of relationship disappointment.

47. "Why does life have to make it easy for you to achieve your goals and accomplish your ends?"
The obvious accurate answer is "It doesn't have to." Leading the client to state the obvious is a good beginning toward dissolving self-pity, dilly-dallying, listlessness, lethargy, and inertia. More anti-procrastinating behavior will likely stem from such an admittance. Seek the client's perspective, e.g.: "What would life be like if you convinced yourself of this idea that life does not have to be made easy for you?" "What advantages would such a view have for you?" Lining up long-term advantages of change in collaboration with the client can be an important cog in motivation for personal change. Perhaps the biggest myth of all time is the creampuff idea that it's easy to take the easy way out. Such a faulty notion encourages demands for ease and comfort cravings while en route to goal achievement.

48. "Why must you feel sorry for yourself when things don't go your way? What good does it do?"
Teaching clients to bend their thinking about the universe rather than thinking they are required to bend the universe in their efforts to not get themselves emotionally bent out of shape brings a more hopeful and humanistic element to the problem-solving process. The revelation that life does *not* have to change before one can feel better is perhaps the most hopeful of all acknowledgments. In rational emotive behavior therapy this is termed the elegant solution, transforming the inner emotional problem without presuming change with the outer, practical concerns; although the client doesn't run the universe he can still control his emotions rather than let emotions control him. Owning up to the often disguised facts of self-pity is no easy task, but it is one that would well be introduced, lest the client get lost in this sea of self-absorption.

49. "Even if you think something is awful, what good does it do to awfulize about it?"

Rational thinking puts special emphasis on anti-awfuliz-ing. "Awful" is a word that contains some degree of exaggeration, therefore it implies that something is beyond reality. Nothing so far as is known is beyond reality. When a client insists that something is "awful," rather than argue the point you can say, "Let's assume that you're right and I'm wrong and that this matter under consideration is awful—what good does it do to awfulize about it?" To use an extreme example, even if we were informed by CNN that there was a nuclear war on the way and that the world was coming to an end in thirty minutes, what good would it do to awfulize about it? Wouldn't we be better off spending the last thirty minutes of our lives by our choosing? Often this line of questioning alerts clients to reconsider using exaggerated terms such as "awful," "terrible," and "horrible," and in doing so, to better regulate their own emotions.

50. "Is there a law of nature that says others have to do the right thing?"
Humans often naturally do the wrong thing. To insist that they be other than the way they are is to invite disturbance. Lobbying for debating the existence of this alleged natural, universal law is a vote for preventing feelings of anger and vindictiveness when associates inevitably do the wrong thing. The human margin for error is very high; proclaiming that others are required to do the right thing goes against this reality dictum.

51. "Do you have a right to be wrong?"
Forgiveness is more likely to take hold when it begins with oneself. Giving oneself emotional slack in the aftermath of wrongdoing makes it much more convenient to forgive others for their trespasses. Being more permissive with self following a mistake sounds simple enough, but because of the human tendency to define oneself by one's errors, it is not an easy thing to do. Since problem-solving will be brought to an all-out standstill until self-condemnation is overcome, until the client is able to vig-

orously self-state that purely and simply, due to free will and human limitations, "I have a right to be wrong," he/she likely will not get out of the self-development starting blocks.

52. "How does it follow that just because others are wrong in being wrong they therefore don't have that right?"
Somewhat humorously relating to the client that "humans have a right to be wrong–they're wrong in being wrong–don't get me wrong–what do you think about what I'm saying?" can be a very light and enlightening manner of breaking down resistances to taking on the more rational and emotionally liberating idea of the human right to be wrong. As with all therapeutic questions, be alert for hedging or qualifying answers that contaminate commitment to a more rational mode of thinking, e.g.: "Others *probably* have a right to be wrong," "I *suppose* they do," "I *guess* they do." Such half-heeded, weak responses had best be brought to the client's attention, e.g.: "You better watch the 'probably,'" "Where does that 'suppose' get you?" "What do you think that 'guess' truly means?" One of the biggest paradoxes of the human condition is that if you ask one thousand people if others have a right to be wrong, practically all would respond affirmatively, "Of course they do!" Yet, when the question is narrowed to "How about *this* person in your life who is frustrating you; does he/she have a right to be wrong?" a vast majority of these same people would likely respond "Of course not!" My point is, humans are not especially hard and fast on simple notions that if not glossed over, but instead accepted more strongly, would better promote emotional stamina. Not letting clients off the hook with their weak, qualifying nontherapeutic responses helps to make therapy a more forceful, empowering experience.

53. "Because it is wrong, does that mean that you or others don't have a choice and can't do it?"
This question is another variation of the theme that is

designed to prompt a verbal response that would result in the client's moving him/herself more solidly toward the idea of freedom of choice—without self- and/or other-damning. Such rational staunchness provides greater peace within and between people.

54. "What are the costs and benefits of your way of thinking?"
Introducing clients to comparative methods of thought is encouraged by suggesting an overview of the emotional consequences of one's value system as expressed in thought and word. Without such a comparative cost analysis, clients are likely to further habituate themselves to rigid, dysfunctional methods of thought. The goal here is to lead the way for clients to illuminate for themselves which ideas would be in their best interest to keep and which would be well to discard. Unless clients can more clearly see for themselves the emotional effects of their belief system, they will continue to put themselves at its mercy.

55. "Because something is undesirable or unbearable, does that mean it shouldn't be?"
Humans have a fancy for exaggerating the significance of things. They strongly lean themselves toward amplifying annoyances. The therapeutic task is to teach them how not to throw gasoline on disappointments. No problem is so small that by doing what comes dramatically naturally, it can't be blown out of proportion. This question is a stepping-stone toward accepting reality, as highly annoying and inconvenient as it often is. Until clients are shown how to lighten up about a problematic world with prob-lematic-acting people, emotional self-control enlighten-ment is unlikely to take place.

56. "When people are disturbing themselves it is because they are demanding something. This demand often comes in the form of a 'must,' 'should,' 'have to' 'ought to,' or 'got to'—what and where is your demand?"
This leading question poses a more active-directive ap-

proach by the therapist. It implies going to the client and honestly getting your hypothesis out on the table for all to see and evaluate. This inquiry gets to the point, at the jugular vein of emotional disturbance–demandingness. Reality is confronted–that until the client curtails raising the roof with his/her unrealistic commands and demands he/she is likely to emotionally suffer. Self-discovery by way of clients' identifying and disputing their own demands is preferable, but when they get themselves bound up in their emotional anguish they are in no shape to make rational conclusions; thus it becomes important to cut through their oversight with frank, direct, persuasive instruction. Actively showing clients their precise "have to" and then giving them the cognitive homework assignment of monitoring themselves by "catching" themselves self-stating this demand, then substituting an "I would like," "I prefer," or "I want," can relieve much emotional pressure. But as I often tell clients, "Don't believe me, try it and find out for yourself!"

57. "When thinking changes, feelings change, so how can you change your thinking to contrast your feelings?"
After clients "get it" regarding the thinking-feeling connection, it is important to impress upon them the value of their responsibility for developing ideas that will result in greater emotional self-reliance. Forthrightly advising clients to think about their thinking, in a way that uses logic and reason in the service of their emotions, is at the base of increasing rational living possibilities.

58. "What feelings/emotions do you think are in the word 'awful'?"
Low frustration tolerance (LFT) is exaggerating the pain that one is required to go through to achieve a given result. Labeling something as "awful" or concluding "I can't stand it" are frequent avenues of giving vent to LFT inclinations. Getting the client to paint him/herself a picture of the unwanted emotional fallout from "awful" expressions can be an encouragement to not lead him/

herself down the garden path in the future. Stress occurs following frustration or inconvenience; distress is brought on by awfulizing about the stressful event.

59.   "What feelings/emotions do you think are in the words 'I can't stand it'?"

Intolerance is at the core of much emotional disturbance. Tolerance deficiencies are often seen in the self-statement "I can't stand it." Getting to the truth of matters is a rational problem-solving ideal. The truth is one can stand anything as long as one is alive. The therapeutic maneuver is to get clients to convince themselves of this reality. Minimizing "I can't stand it" in one's vocabulary will decrease tension and increase contentment. Leading clients to identify the feelings of malcontent flowing from these four stress-producing words sets the stage for asking them (a) if they want to feel emotionally lighter and (b) if they wish to explore other beliefs that would hold more promise for stressless living. Once you get the green light from them, indicating they want to lighten up emotionally and are willing to consider options in doing so, ask them what better conclusions might be drawn about frustration, and give them a few suggestions of your own. Examples could include:

"I don't like this turn of events."
"These matters of life and love are disappointing."
"How regrettable that the world and some of the people in it are not bending in my favor."
"Sadness prevails now that this major inconvenience has occurred."

Until the "I-can't-stand-it-itis" is minimized, hopelessness will dominate until "I can't stand it" as basically a declaration that the individual couldn't possibly make him/herself happier until what he/she allegedly "can't stand" is made to go away. A client recently said, "I can't stand living." Thinking that I should check that statement out for any suicidal ideation that might lie behind it, I asked, "Do you have any thoughts of suicide?"

The client responded, "No, I couldn't stand dying." This is the message behind this intolerant philosophy, that the facts of living and dying are unbearable—but what is there then left to play with?

60. "Is the result of possible failure so earthshaking that you are unwilling to risk everything and guarantee failure by not trying?"
Gaining better results usually requires some changes. Because we live in a world that is random, objective, and impartial there is the ever-present chance factor to contend with. The biggest risk of all is to habitually play it close to the vest. If one comes out of the dugout and gets into the game, he will win some and lose some. If he stays in the dugout he will seldom win in the game of life. This challenging question is designed to get the client to see that there is little gain without pain or risk and that there is an entry fee for deciding to try, that fee being the discomfort that is made to accompany the uncertain trek into the unknown. This question implies that considering failure as bigger than life and the worst of all possible crimes should be reconsidered.

61. "What does mental resistance and mental karate mean for you and what can they do for you?"
After explaining to a seven-year-old boy the ABCs of "mental karate" regarding his emotions in the face of peer ridicule, he stated, "Oh, do you mean mental resistance?" Novel terms, upon being defined and understood, can help to recall important principles of emotional self-control; you have power over how you feel through how you think.

62. "Do you think that it makes any difference in how a person feels when he says 'I want,' 'would like,' 'wish,' 'desire,' 'prefer,' rather than 'I've got to,' 'have to,' 'need to,' 'should,' 'must'?"
Drawing out contrasting emotions behind contrasting thoughts is an ongoing process whose purpose is to, with each question, strengthen the idea that the thoughts one

chooses largely determine one's emotions. Simple re-alignments in one's thinking can make a major difference in how one feels. By repeatedly bringing this to the clients' attention, in that repetition is the mother of learning, it is more likely to sink in for the advantages of their emotional well-being. Little things, especially when persistently repeated over time, can mean a lot. Little is so powerful as an idea whose time has come. Asking questions that keep simple, nondemanding, tolerant ideas out on the table increases the chances that they will be ingested and digested in a manner that will serve emotional nutrition well.

63. "What do you think are some of your thoughts that lead to excessive emotional problems?"
Getting at the thoughts that create unwanted feelings of shame, embarrassment, guilt, rage, etc., is preferably done in direct collaboration with the client. Two heads are often better than one in efforts to get to the same side of the table and fight the problem of unscientific, illogical thinking.

64. "How can you not put yourself down for your errors, yet still fully acknowledge them?'"
Accountability for one's behavior is perhaps the first step in personal change. This can be more efficiently done by instructing the client to not combine fault and blame. Fault is to do wrong; blame is to condemn yourself for your fault. Acknowledgment of and accountability for your errors without acceptance of yourself for committing them spells (a) emotional disturbance and (b) a blockage of problem-solving in that if you put yourself down for having faults, you will be too busy doing just that to correct them. Getting clients to instill in themselves "Acknowledgment, accountability, and correction, yes! Condemnation, no!" is a difficult task because they assume that fault and blame are automatically a package deal, that if you identify your faults you naturally have to berate yourself for having them. Because of

this erroneous idea, humans are often not willing to di-
vulge their deficiencies. When they see that accountability for self does not mean condemning of self, they will
feel more comfortable in admitting to their blunders and
shortcomings.

65. "How can you not put others down for their errors and
still acknowledge yet protect yourself from their mistakes?"
This question is the flip side of the previous one and
promotes responsible self-expression—telling someone
how you feel without telling them off. Putting yourself
down causes depression, shame, and/or guilt. Putting others down will cause you anger. The end result of this line
of questioning is intended for the client to become more
assertive and self-directed and less aggressive or nonas-
sertive in his/her behavior. Like practically all goals, the
idea of responsible self-expression can better be accomplished with a clear head. Getting the client to see the
value of not putting down a difficult acting person so as
to avoid tunnel-visioned anger, yet expressing the dis-
taste that he/she has for another's deplorable actions, is
the clear-thinking, more sanely acting follow-up intent of
this question.

66. "Do you have to accept and take on another's criticisms
or putdowns? How could you not do this if you chose not
to?"
This inquiry and its follow-up seek to counter a common
misery equation: "others' opinions = me." When clients
are introduced to understand *and* strongly convince
themselves that they are not at the mercy of another's
view, they often appreciatively and adventurously seek
out varied manners of expression and experience that
they previously blocked, out of their overconcern about
what others might think about them if they failed. After
clients acknowledge that they don't have to buy into
another's critical comments, they can (preferably) lead
themselves or (if not able to do so) be led into the cogni-

tive correlates of accepting themselves regardless of others' views of them. Such adamant adopted philosophies could include: "Others' opinions reflect their tastes and preferences, not mine." "I've got better things to do than sharpen up others' sticks and stones to stick into myself!" "I don't need others' approval and favoritism to begin with!" "Others cannot emotionally hurt me; only I can hurt myself by taking their comments personally."

67. "How could you keep from putting yourself down just because others attempt to?"
Like number 66 this question directs clients to the emotionally liberating idea that all putdowns are self-inflicted—no one can put you down but you. Others can select and discriminate against you but a putdown can follow only if *you* define yourself by the other person's opinion. This follows Eleanor Roosevelt's philosophy that "No one can make you feel inferior unless you give them permission."

68. "Do you think it is the shape of the road or how you walk it that counts more?"
Guiding the client further toward becoming his/her own best counselor can be gradually accomplished with repeated questions that reflect the philosopher Epitetus' statement of two thousand years ago: "People don't get disturbed by events, but the views which they take of events." Humans are affected by the shape of their road in life but it is their demandingness that such a shape not exist, e.g., "It shouldn't be so hard," "It must not be," "Things oughta be different," and their exaggeration of the significance of its shape, e.g., "It's too hard," "I can't stand it," "What a bummer," that create disturbance. Solutions to emotional problems that interfere with human happiness are philosophical and the development of questions that encourage clients to be more philosophical about and to develop a philosophy of their concerns that is compatible with their mental health should be integrated into the interview process.

69. "Is it worth it for you to work hard on your problems?"
Clients often comment on how difficult it is to short-circuit dysfunctional thoughts, feelings, and behaviors that have become habitual. When a client whiningly states "But it's so hard to change," it is important to dart into the conversation and quickly steer it into a more hopeful direction by asking "Would it be worth it?" Once acknowledgment that it would be worth it to change is gained, particular details as to why it would be worth it can be sought. This line of pursuance is based on a therapeutic ideal of maneuvering the client into convincing *you* why it is in his/her best interest to change. Achieving this ideal moves away from the all-too-frequent occurrence of the counselor's frustrating him/herself by trying to transplant motivation while talking the client into changing.

70. "Do you think that others' advantages make them better than you?"
Humans are not born equal; some are born with more advantages than others. Those with more advantages, e.g., more intelligence, financial inheritance, physical prowess, or natural handsomeness or beauty, have more of a jump on life and are therefore better off. However, there is a major distinction between being better off and being a better person. Will Rogers said, "It's great to be great; it's even better to be human." This question examines the rational philosophy of the unrateability of human beings—that there is merit in rating characteristics, traits, and performances but pernicious side effects from rating the people who have them. "Judge behaviors, not people" is the message behind this question. When clients are directly taught that their comparative disadvantages mean they're worse off but not a worse person, they are likely to less anxiously be able to secure more advantages.

71. "Do you think that it follows that people always have to do what they are capable of doing?"
The sky is not the limit by way of human potential. There

is a ceiling and there is a floor. It is wise to want to do well within this ceiling and floor. But because something is better doesn't mean a person has to do it. This question is meant to illuminate a very basic distinction between sanity and emotional disturbance–sorting out being preferentially motivated from being demandingly insistent. To suggest to oneself a desire to do well is wise; to demand that one always, under all conditions, must apply maximum potential in doing so is self-defeating. To get clients to try on their own behalf is one thing; for them to insist on maximum capability in doing so is quite another. This perfectionistic insistence will discourage reasonable effort with its tiring effort to demandingly do the impossible.

72. "What do you think might happen if you stopped trying to change/convince the other person that he is wrong and instead started to learn how to better tolerate his shortcomings, accepting him the way he is?"
Getting the client to adopt a philosophy of "I'll change," not "I'll change you" is the essence of good relationship counseling. Issuing a line of questioning that sensibly reflects a "my dear, how you've changed since I've changed" philosophy pursues the idea of implementing more individual responsibility for self in relationship problems. Such individual emphasis for change takes much pressure off the parties involved that stems from trying to do the impossible–change another human being. The mood becomes more tempered and (self-) reflective following this gently confrontive question.

73. "Would you lie to/mistrust you if you were your significant other?"
In an effort to get one partner to assume more responsibility for relationship disruption, it is often helpful to ask that person to walk a mile in the other person's moccasins, gain a sense for what that is like, and see if she too would find it convenient to be deceitful and to mistrust herself. An affirmative response can be quite revealing and humbling, encouraging less blame and friction. Real-

izing that when told the truth in the past she overreacted to it, and that when counted upon, her reliability factor fell through, can provide a glimpse of her role in what the deceitfulness and questioning is about.

74. "What can you better do to keep your emotional shirt on?"
Giving the client many opportunities to respond to questions that imply he/she digs in by way of refusing to get him/herself emotionally disturbed about disappointments can pay eventual therapeutic dividends. Brainstorming with the client what those options are allows the counselor to intersect with the client in a unique and meaningful way—as a partnership against the common enemy of emotional disturbance.

75. "Why are your values sacred and why must others not oppose them?"
Humans have one dickens of a time figuring out how others can think differently than they. Perhaps the biggest challenge facing the human condition is learning how to respect individual differences. It seems that practically all humans think they know the absolute truth about certain things. "My way," "the way," and "the *only* way" is the battle cry of the true believer. Educating clients about the emotional pitfalls of absolutist thinking is a valued enterprise. Until the client is instructed as to the value of their values and how to take the sacredness out of their values, emotional health will take a back seat. Questions that lead into countering all-or-nothing, dichotomous thinking often pay off when the client begins to appreciate the enormous amount of emotional relief that is gained from desacredizing one's beliefs.

76. "When life isn't fair, isn't that all the more reason to be fair to yourself?"
It is a given of the human condition to be treated unfairly much of the time. However, all is not lost in that one can always be fair to oneself. In fact, when life isn't fair this may be all the more reason to be fair to oneself, if in no other way than by not taking a bad situation and making

it worse. When clients learn to accept that they get what they get and not what's fair, they begin to blossom more emotionally.

77. "Why shouldn't things be a certain way just because you don't like them that way?"
Grandiosity is a cornerstone of emotional disturbance. Disputing the notion that "I am the center of the universe, and everything that I want must be, and everything that I don't want must not be" creates a rude awakening in the short run but helps you to sleep better at night in the long run. Abolishing self-centeredness is often at center stage in problem-solving planning. Directing clients away from infantile demands for preferential treatment makes for more realistic problem-solving possibilities. By directly and persuasively getting the client to accept reality as it is, rather than protest against its existence, you reflect Ziggy's hypothesis about his own problems and disturbances: "My problem is that I like things as they aren't." Abruptly dispelling "the world exists for me" misconceptions better induces sleep by reducing the stress and tension that filters from grandiose demands.

78. "What are some things that you can do to help you to remember to do what is in your best interests?"
There is a difference between knowing something and using something. All the good talking therapy in the world is rendered useless unless applied in daily living. Questions that cue clients into tying a string around their finger as a reminder to put to use what information they are learning in their counseling increases the chances that a transfer of learning, from the not-so-sacred therapy hour to the other 167 hours of the week, will take place. This question puts the responsibility on clients to implement the behavioral component of their therapy. Examples of aids that increase the chances of remembering to apply ideas generated include getting a special "therapy folder" to keep notes about the therapy and readings assigned as part of the therapy, placing reminders on the

bathroom mirror, e.g., "It's not what I know that is as important as what I do with what I know–now what am I going to do today that will address not what can my therapy do for me but what can I do for my therapy?" penalizing oneself, e.g., getting up two hours earlier the next morning if a week goes by without doing at least three self-interested things that branch off your therapy.

79. "Is it what happened to you or your translation of what happened to you that is more of a problem?"
The truth of the matter often gets lost in the translation. Clients draw conclusions about their life experiences and then keep those original mind-sets alive rather than scientifically assess them by asking themselves: "That was my interpretation at the time, now where is the evidence that my hunch now is, or was ever, correct for that matter?" One of the primary goals of cognitive-behavior therapists is to get their clients to examine their interpretation of what events mean for them, for it is that meaning and not the event itself that causes emotional disturbance. Until cognitive distortions are corrected, the behavioral component of change will be made more difficult.

80. "Why do you think it is that one person 'needs' to be understood and another doesn't?"
Emotional dependency is perhaps the most common problem known to humans. It is usually expressed in the form of a "need," e.g., "I need certain things from others, and when they don't grant me what I need, they destroy me–those shitheads!" This question begins to introduce the idea that individuals are not at the mercy of others' understanding. It is important to get at the specific self-sentences, then promote their use, e.g., "Another's understanding does not equal me, so therefore I don't have to stand myself in judgment according to whether others understand me or not"; "Understanding is a very nice thing, but is not necessary; better that I not necessitize about something that is important." As clients begin to talk themselves out of "needing" others' understand-

ing, they are likely to more pleasantly lubricate their relationships with their social group.

81. "What do you think would be the benefits of your not depending on someone else's approval?"
Much of what is called (disapproval) anxiety is an over-concern about what others might think about us. This question begins to identify manners of thought that can loosen up rather than tighten up knots in the gut that stem from fretting about others' disapproval. Loosening up the frozen judgment that "I need others' approval" begins by listing and pursuing countering thoughts, e.g., "It's great when others approve of me, but my life doesn't depend on it," "I can get through the night, preferably with, but also disappointedly without, others' approval," "Disapproval is bad but I'm not bad when subjected to it nor are others evil for subjecting me to it." Enabling the client to experience the benefits of emotional well-being by adopting and acting upon such flexible philosophies is the hoped-for outcome of this planted question.

82. "Wouldn't it be better for you to draw your own conclusions apart from what others might think is best for you?"
Thoreau indicated that "a single person can constitute a majority of one." Thinking for oneself about what is best for you, rather than giving blind adherence to what others, e.g., parents, teachers, ministers, friends–all of whom have problems of their own–think that you "should," "must," or "ought to" do, is a rational therapeutic goal.

83. "Does your value to yourself and your valued existence hinge upon others?"
Contained in this question is the signal to clients that there are things that they can practically always do, regardless of circumstance, e.g., accept themselves, count on themselves, and find meaning in their lives. So is teaching them that it is not that others don't count, rather it's that they don't count in an essential, all-or-nothing way. The more your line of questioning promotes thera-

peutic direction that highlights emotional self-reliance, the better. Such a self-sufficient focus allows you to help more clients, more often, in shorter periods of time.

84. **"Can others betray your deepest values?"**
A recent client who had been severely physically abused by his parents as a child was quickly able to find it in his head and heart to identify their right to be wrong and consequently forgave them for being wrong in their initial abuse. However, what he gave himself difficulty with was his refusal to accept their right to not learn from their original mistake (even after the child welfare authorities had intervened and corrected them) and instead repeatedly continue to beat him even after they were told and knew better. One of this client's deepest values was "others must learn from their mistakes." He refused to accept the reality that his parents obviously didn't learn from theirs and that this disproved his hypothesis that they "must." As a result he continued to make himself feel hurt, angry, and betrayed. Assigning clients the task of spending a few minutes each day to actively forgive their adversaries for betraying their deepest values enhances emotional relief.

85. **"Can it be proven that you are diminished as a human being if someone else thinks less of you?"**
Second fiddle does not mean second class. Each time clients are asked to produce empirical data to support their hypotheses, e.g., if someone else thinks less of them they are therefore a lesser person, they gradually establish a healthier sense of skepticism. Challenging and changing beliefs that you have steadfastly held is not always comforting at first, but as George Bernard Shaw said, "Because a true believer appears happier than a skeptic is no more to the point than a drunk appears happier than a sober person." Well-rehearsed faulty beliefs that smack of diminishment of self are difficult to relinquish but are even more difficult to cling to. Because of the emotional relief that follows, clients often are

grateful when a less dependent perspective is introduced; this question begins to pave the way to do just that.

86. "Do you have value to yourself apart from your successes, performances, achievements, and accomplishments?"

When clients can be induced to answer "Come to think of it I do!" their emotional relief quotient goes up. Success as the gateway to the kingdom of God puts pressure on those feverishly trying to raise the entry fee. Steer clients away from the "rating game," in which they give themselves a report card with a good mark for their successful performances and accomplishments, and the same report card with a bad mark for their failings and flounderings. This "game" causes emotions to fluctuate, with clients giving themselves bad cases of emotional seasickness. Doing well in some ways results in feeling better. Yet, worrying about continuing to do well lest one turn back into a "bad" person in the event one should falter results in getting worse because of the inevitability of failure. Getting clients to answer this question by explaining to you that they do their performances but are not their performances, and consequently have value to themselves apart from their works, stimulates an emotional breath of fresh air.

87. "Do people have a right to do things that you don't like? Why or why not?"

People can be bothersome when they act in annoying, undesirable ways. Inasmuch as nothing between any two humans is ideal, it is important to enter relationships armed with cognitions that don't amplify grievances. These twin questions are designed to ward off human tendencies to escalate disappointments into disturbances. This type of asking allows client and counselor to put their heads together and identify client-invented ways of looking at the world that require others to make life more convenient for the client to be happier by patronizing his/her values.

88. "Because others blame you, do you have to blame your-self? How could you not do this if you chose not to?"
Attaching these questions together is another method of getting clients to retrain themselves in a more self-ac-cepting, emotionally independent direction. Turning the light bulb on for clients to see that they are not duty bound to imitate their aggressors helps in not duplicating others' judgments while not compounding annoyance into emotional disturbance. Bringing out the ideas that "others' opinions do *not* equal me and because I faulted and because others blame me for my mistake does *not* mean that I must blame myself" is the objective of this question.

89. "What are some ways for you to tolerate something that you don't like?"
Brainstorming what will help clients to tolerate what they don't like is an asset for containing emotional disruption. Tactics of cognitive distraction, e.g., pushing out of mind the troublesome situation or the feelings in it; behavioral distractions, e.g., engaging in various pleasures that help "take your mind off it"; realigning your life circum-stance so that it is more to your liking, e.g., finding a higher-quality job; revamping philosophies of life, e.g., "I *can* stand what I don't like" are all fodder for possibi-lities during a how-to-make-oneself-more-tolerant think-tank session. Clients often convince themselves that they can't put up with various displeasures. The backbone of this question is that it begins to search for ways to de-velop patience and high frustration tolerance. In a world in which it often takes twenty or more years to become an overnight success, a world that contains an abundance of pleasures often not within reach, such lofty goals are nothing to sneeze at.

90. "Do you always, or for that matter ever, have to do what is for the best?"
Humans often subscribe to the idea that they have to do what is for the best. This irrational conclusion puts their

mental health generally, and their self-acceptance specifically, far from reach. Instructing clients of the desirability
of contributing to their long-range happiness and survival, without demanding that they do so at all times,
prevents the solution from being transformed into the
problem. "Have to" philosophies cause cringes in the
gut; "want to" ideas create solutions in the head. This
question is aimed at not putting the cart before the horse;
by taking pressure off themselves by understanding that
they aren't required to change, clients make it more likely
that they will change—in a more clearheaded way to boot!

91. "Why do you need to control anything or anyone?"
    Most humans have a not-so-secret ambition to run the
    universe. This question is a stepping-stone to giving up
    such impossible ventures. It seeks to pique the client's
    interest in exploring the idea that by giving up on the
    something or somebody the client will gain more control.
    Its intent is not to give up on striving for what one wants
    or on influencing others but instead to do so in a nondic-
    tatorial way. This question also gets at the emotional
    dependency that lies behind controlling futilities. Using
    this question as a lead can show the client not only that he
    doesn't need to control anything or anyone but that he
    can achieve even fuller emotional emancipation by see-
    ing that he doesn't need anything or anyone—in fact, he
    doesn't even need to survive—he *chooses* to do so. Such
    an elastic perspective helps to increase control for greater
    personal health and happiness.

92. "Do you think that this matter is part of life or bigger
    than life?"
    By addressing the distinction between matters that are a
    part of life and those considered to be bigger than life, the
    client is provided options of thoughts and feelings. Ques-
    tions such as this allow clients to discover finer-tuned
    outlooks that better service their emotional well-being.
    Asking the client to describe the advantages of such a

differential perspective incorporates further her involvement in her understanding about helping herself.

93. "Why would you not risk failure, disapproval, and being wrong?"

"Because failure, disapproval, and being wrong are awful and I'd be awful for getting myself caught up in them" would be the common answer to this question. This inquiry tries to reveal the twin towers of emotional disturbances–intolerance of these and other unpleasantries and self-downing for perceived deficiencies in coping with them. Prompting clients to open up about what these activated adversities mean for them is a beginning step in changing their tune about them. If clients have difficulty answering the original inquiry, suggest possible meanings they attach to failure, disapproval, and being wrong, e.g.:

"Aren't you really telling yourself they are awful and that you're vile for getting yourself caught up in them?"
"Is it possible that . . ."
"My suspicion is that . . ."
"Would it be fair to say that . . ."
"Sometimes people tell themselves _____ about such matters; are you?"

Sharing your hypotheses with clients about their possible conclusions permits a convergence of focus on the problems at hand.

94. "Do you believe that it is really a catastrophe if others don't like or understand you?"

Going into a social situation, most people believe it would be an absolute horror if they were not liked or understood. Such a tumultuous perspective often brings on what the person fears, e.g., by exaggerating the significance of others' not finding you compatible with them, you are likely to unnerve yourself about the possibility of such dire happenings, bringing on their dislike. Earmarking anti-catastrophic philosophies that can be generalized to practically any unwanted life circumstance is the essence of the logic behind this question, e.g., "this is sad but not tragic," "difficult but not unbearable," "regretful but not horrible," "hard but not too hard."

95. "How would you like to be a little different a week from now?"
     The essence of good therapy is homework assignments. Not more insight but application to daily living is what matters most as an offshoot of therapy. To identify specific changes the client would like to make and to assign homework commensurate with these changes cultivates hope, anticipation, and participation.

96. "Based on what we have talked about today, what do you think would be a good homework assignment for you to give yourself?"
     Engaging the client in the activity component of his therapy creates less resistance because clients are less likely to resist their own suggestions. Making clients an active part of their own treatment puts more responsibility for self-focus on the project.

97. "What did you learn from doing the homework that you assigned yourself?"
     This question indicates that life and therapy are for lessons and that it is anticipated that the client will learn a few. Creating a climate of education of self, based on the experiences the client has, indicates that when school is in session, learning is likely to occur. This question also strikes upon the idea of therapy as a personal science in which clients are encouraged, if not expected, to get a data base in order to confirm or disconfirm their original hypothesis. Clients have preconceived ideas about what certain decisions or circumstances mean for them, and the trick and treatment is to test out those hunches via direct exposure to them. Implementing heavy doses of exposure therapy in which clients push themselves to try different things first and draw conclusions second, rather than the other way around, almost always results in their being better off for the learning.

98. "What would be the advantages of your taking your fears and other discomforts with you?"

    "Nothing ventured, nothing gained" is the byword of this question. Until clients accept their queasiness as the price they pay for doing something different, little benefit will be gained. Familiarity with a project blunts the seeming terrors of doing it. Discussing with clients the advantages of forcing themselves to the task—whether they feel like it or not—is done in the aftermath of this asking.

99. "Would you have the same problem if you were with someone else?"

    Humans tend to think that if they were to switch associates (e.g., lovers, co-workers, friends, relatives) their problems and disturbances would go away. Little do they realize that their personalizations and overreactions are part of general problems they have and will continue to have, regardless of who they are with, until they realize that they have met the enemy—and the enemy is them. This question leads into a discussion of the realities of associating with imperfect people in an imperfect world; people are different and differences tend to clash—until you develop a decent respect for the differences. This moderately confronting question also helps to assess clients' capacity to look within themselves to examine their own part in the problem-development plot.

100. "What do you think are some better ways of getting people's attention besides getting yourself angry?"

    This question hits on the anti-collaborative nature of anger. It expects people to think of alternative, less dramatic methods of coming together to communicate, cooperate, and compromise. Identifying civilized methods of relating is the desired outcome of this question.

101. "Did he/she get you angry or did you make yourself angry about what he/she did?"

    Consistently bringing clients back to the reality of their responsibility for their own thoughts, emotions, and behaviors is one of the main goals of therapy. This question promotes that responsibility for self-focus.

102. "Do you think that one person can really take away another person?"
Humans tend magically to think that one person can emotionally whisk away another. This question attempts to begin to point out that when one person treats another person with high doses of encouragement, respect, understanding, and acceptance the desire to leave that person is far less likely to occur. The goal of this question is to establish a recognition that no one can steal another's partner without consent, and the will to move on is less likely to develop with the establishment of the above pleasantries.

103. "What is it about your relationship that would encourage your partner to want to be with someone else in the first place?"
Defining what pricklies the worrisome partner might be interjecting into the relationship alerts him/her to the degree of responsibility he/she has for the incompatible state of the relationship. This question can nicely lead into a discussion about how more flies are ordinarily caught with honey than with vinegar.

104. "If your partner and you were to select different mates, who do you think would have a greater difficulty in the new relationships?"
Good therapeutic questions attempt to reveal information that, when gathered and applied, results in clients' living more of the kind of life they would like to have. This question attempts to look down the road and provide a glimpse of how rocky it might be in an effort to create motivation for relationship change in the present. Difficulties abound in almost any relationship, and some of the current ones might be a fair trade-off for future ones. This manner of inquiry attempts to illuminate that present-to-future comparison and contrast.

105. "Do you have to take others' unkind treatment and turn it into an insult?"
All insults are self-inflicted. No one can insult you but you. Demeaningness is a state of mind and no one can give a state of mind to another. This question leads into a discussion that no one can transplant a belief into another's head or a feeling into another's gut and how such an affirmation of free-will perspective allows you to *not* automatically respond to others' ill-willed behaviors.

106. "How can you better influence others to respond to you rather than you mainly responding to them?"
This question considers communication as a two-way street. Assertive means of gaining another's attention can be discussed within the context of preferably doing so in a straightforward, clearheaded way. Interdependence in relating to another can be better established by collaborating on a plan that emphasizes the value of give and take, rotation and balance in listening to another and in being listened to by another. Such communication might include making an assertive position statement, e.g., "I believe . . ."; using prepared statements, e.g., "I don't like what you just said"; passing along a well-thought-out note, e.g., "Dear _____, I want to tell you _____"; or behavioral trade-offs whereby the client declares "I won't do what you want me to do (scratch your back), until you do what I want you to do (scratch my back)."

107. "Did you use poor judgment or did you use good judgment but fail to act on it?"
This question reveals the distinction between a thinking or talking decision and a doing decision. Its aftermath discussion centers on the value of risk taking and countering the demand for the surety and certainty of a favorable outcome when using one's own judgment. It also leads into the value of trusting oneself to stand behind what one deems to be one's wisest choice.

108. "Did you make the wrong decision or a decision based on present evidence?"

This question tries to pave the way toward getting rid of insistence on knowing tomorrow's answers today. Decisions can be made only with present evidence in hand. The handwriting on the wall may change from one day to the next; it's the demanding to try to tie present evidence in with a guaranteed future outcome that makes for confusion. When clients are taught the value of basing choices on what is happening rather than what might happen in the future, they are less likely to halt upon the brink of a decision. Freeing themselves from searching for a "right" decision saves time and frustration by permitting more decisive decision making. This question illustrates the general principle that it takes a long time to find something that doesn't exist, in this case a "right" answer.

109. "Do you want to feel better now or better for the rest of your life?"
      Clients should be encouraged to take a long-range view of life. This question helps to expose the low frustration tolerance behind approaching life in a shortsighted way. Upon approaching a fork in the decision-making road, a decision is to be made that reflects the options of feeling better today, e.g., setting oneself down to rest to avoid the toil required to accomplish something that would contribute to your long-range happiness and survival, or feeling better in the long run by attending to the matter of concern, now. This question takes center aim at the value of making short-run sacrifices for long-run gain; present pain for future gain. Getting clients to see beyond their own noses is a central goal of problem-solving in that, until they do take on philosophies of effort that reflect "doing gets it done," "no time like the present," or "the line of least resistance is oftentimes the line of most resistance," they will likely refuse to put themselves through the hard work that often precedes personal change.

110. "Do you think that it would be fair to others if they were required to accept your values?"
      "Save time—see it my way" is the belief that is at the base

of many relationship problems. This question squarely faces the undemocratic view that others' values must be a clone of yours. Getting the client to acknowledge the value of and to act upon a more liberal perspective injects a healthy amount of emotional slack into his/her interpersonal relationships.

111. "Would it be better for you to not be involved and not make mistakes or be involved and feel comforted upon making mistakes because that shows you are trying and learning?"

Once clients appreciate that failure isn't bigger than life, they ordinarily free themselves to try different life possibilities that they have resisted seeking. When failure is seen as an advantage rather than as shattering, much trying, failing, learning and oftentimes eventually succeeding takes place. Getting the client to explain to you his/her view regarding the obvious answer to this question is an important step in his/her doing more and stewing less.

112. "Do you believe that it is mandatory that you not be frustrated, deprived, and inconvenienced?"

Inconveniences sacredized equal emotional disturbance. Developing with clients a philosophy of frustration and discomfort that is compatible with their mental health has its beginnings in this question. It helps to promote the reality that apparently we are not in this world to feel comfortable, but rather to experience the world and its discomforts. Less avoidance of difficult but important long-range tasks is likely to follow from spearheading this more tolerant view.

113. "Is it really essential that you know tomorrow's answers today and what disadvantages would befall you if you did?"

Looking at the realities behind insistences can be quite revealing. The closer one looks at a goal, the more tarnished it is likely to become. Clients are usually amused when informed that if tomorrow's answers were known today, life would be quite drab. This interesting insight can help clients to take themselves less seriously in relation to their unrealistic demand of knowing today what is going to happen tomorrow. Being glad that one is not in the know of tomorrow's answers today helps to lessen the common fear of the unknown. Being rich has problems, just as being poor does, and knowing tomorrow's answers today can have as many problems as not knowing them. A life without anticipation is a life with less participation.

114. "What is the worst thing that could follow 'what if' and why could you not tolerate it if it did occur?"
When clients don't come to terms with their ability to cope with their biggest fear, they will likely startle themselves with the self-sentence "What if it occurs–wouldn't that be awful?" This question introduces to and tries to sell the client on the value of higher-level problem solving. Rationally coming to terms with failure, disapproval, and/or discomfort by convincing oneself that such disappointments are not disasters permits a fuller breath of emotional fresh air. Success, approval, and comfort are redefined as nice, but not necessary. Control for them is still seen as preferable, but not essential. When clients are led to dispute their irrational beliefs about dissatisfactions, and more sensibly conclude that they are not shattering or dreadful after all, they often find it more convenient to open themselves to new life experiences. On the other hand, "what if" opens up the floodgates to anxiety because it implies that everything and anything could catastrophically happen.

115. "Would it be better for you to not care, or to care less without becoming uncaring?"
Humans tend to go to extremes in their thinking, from "I-can't-stand-it-itis," in which they actively convince themselves that they absolutely cannot do or go without something, to "I-don't-give-a-shit-itis," in which they loudly con themselves into thinking that not doing or going without something is a piece of cake. Educating

them on the value of being concerned about not being able to engage themselves in their desires, but not consuming themselves about such deprivations, helps them to maintain a more balanced mood. Between caring too much about something and not caring at all is the happier medium of caring less without becoming uncaring. This philosophy enables clients to affirm their values in a more balanced way. A common belief is if you don't get yourself emotionally entangled in your concerns you will stop emoting. This is far from accurate. Just because a person does away with interfering emotions, e.g., anger, guilt, fear, rage, fury, doesn't mean that person stops feeling. Rather, caring less paves the way for more wholesome emotions that increase enjoyment in life.

116.   "What do you think of the idea 'Take the sacredness out of your values and you will take much emotional disturbance out of your life'?"
De-establishing golden rules is a primary thrust of cognitive-behavior therapy. In line with George Bernard Shaw's position, "The only golden rule is—there is no golden rule," rational-thinking principles try to abandon absolutes in that it is an all-or-nothing, this-way-or-that type perspective that lays the foundation of emotional disturbance. Clients come to therapy with their golden rules related to how they think they and others (including their therapist) should, must, have to, or ought to be. When such sacredness is inevitably violated, the client will distress him/herself. This question begins to encourage clients to identify and appreciate their values without making them out to be bigger than life.

117.   "Do you think that it would be awful or highly inconvenient if you failed?"
Presenting clients with food for thought that will help lead to constructive action on behalf of their lives is the primary purpose of asking rational questions. Unless inconvenience is, through questions, distinguished from

catastrophe, clients will be unlikely to risk failure, and consequently seldom succeed.

118. "Does the past haunt you or do you haunt yourself about the past?"
Humans invent ideas, then keep them alive. This question can lead into a discussion that shows clients that they are responsible for originally interpreting and then renewing interpretations of past happenings. Past events have virtually nothing to do with the emotional disturbances of today; present overreactive, personalized conclusions about former occurrences do.

119. "What do you think is more important—what you think about you or what other people think about you?"
This question makes curtailing disapproval anxiety fair game. In that much of what is called anxiety is an over-concern about what others might think about us, this is an important hunt. As clients discover that their views of self can override others' veto of them, they begin to approach life more assertively and less defensively.

120. "Who do you think is ultimately responsible for one's emotions?"
Interjecting questions that increase the likelihood of getting answers that acknowledge responsibility for self is an ongoing effort. Because humans have a marked tendency to attribute their unwanted emotions to unwanted outside factors, this is a task where persistence against odds can pay off.

121. "Of all the things we have discussed today, what do you remember the most?"
Tracking the client's learning checkpoints by asking this question prior to concluding the session has two main advantages. First, it alerts clients that they are expected to learn something(s) from their therapy while conveying that they are expected to remember what that is. As a result of this question, clients are more likely to "listen up" in future sessions, knowing that they are going to be held accountable for highlighting meeting content. Gain-

ing and maintaining attentiveness is part and parcel of meeting and beating client resistances, and this question is part of what helps to do so. Second, the question gives you feedback as to what ideas are especially helpful for your clients. Such data can be applied with future clients, with similar problems.

122. "What do you think of the idea that there is more strength in laughter than there is in tears?"
A common denominator of emotional disturbance is that the individual is taking him/herself way too seriously—enter humor. Ethel Barrymore said, "You grow up after your first laugh–at yourself." A good assessment and treatment tool is to observe and encourage the client's ability to laugh at self. Humor allows for an enjoyable way to use oneself to get past clients' resistance to change. The last thing a downtrodden client needs is to be taken too seriously. Both counselor and client benefit by inserting humor into the discussion about the grim facts of life. Because humor builds bridges and makes it convenient for others to gravitate toward us, it helps to facilitate collaboration with, and the cooperation of, the client.

123. "What do you think of the idea that, as hard as certain things that are good for you are to do, they are harder not to do?"
Extending client's often-heard statement about an otherwise therapeutic task, "But that's so hard to do," by asking this long-term reality question can get clients to see past the pleasure of the moment—that often leads to pain later on. Much therapy is getting clients to see that procrastinating will defeat them in the long haul, that it is not easy to do the wrong thing. When clients see there is a piper to pay, that the future's chickens will come home to roost, they will be more inclined to examine and change their slackened-effort ways.

124. "What does the idea that 'the past doesn't get any better' mean for you?"
Magical thinking has it that if a person broods and stews

about something unfortunate that has happened, that occurrence will be made better. Getting clients to accept that the past is without a future promotes a more hopeful perspective about what can still be made rather than agonize about what has happened and cannot be changed.

125. "What do you think is more important, your past or what you can bring to your present and future?"
One of the best remedies for the deficiencies of the past is creating efficiencies in the present and future. An array of questions that highlight a focus on today and tomorrow takes the wind out of the sails of the yesteryears.

126. "What do you think of the idea that anything you believe, you can disbelieve?"
Encouraging clients to find value in questioning and changing their beliefs when it would be in their best interest to do so is a major goal of cognitive-behavior therapy. Exercise of free will is a significant therapeutic happening that can occur when clients are led to see their ability to do so.

127. "What do you think of the idea that you can learn manners from those who have none?"
Clients often overestimate the negative influence of "poor role models" in their lives. This question provides a different, unconventional twist to human imitativeness. Taking something bad and turning it into an advantage can be a predominant part of the helping process. Negative-acting models can be a major source of emotional and behavioral revenue in that they teach "how not to do it" by their irrational thinking, feeling, and behavioral ways of approaching life. *If* they play their cards right, clients can choose to take a different life's track than did their predecessors and predators. Clients who have been abused as children and have been fervently lamenting about these experiences find it especially refreshing to take a more well-rounded perspective to the original adversity. By using the therapeutic content behind this question, those who have been abused can learn the value

of not abusing others; those who have been subject to significant others' alcoholic ways as children can better gauge their own relationship with alcohol.

128. "Is your enemy the past, or how you think about and overreact to the past?"
Individuals and their interpretation of the past are the culprit of emotional disturbance, not the past itself. The sooner and more strongly clients see and accept that, the better. Identifying with the client those specific self-sentences that bring on upset about the past paves the way for the challenging and changing of such irrational notions.

129. "When you act badly, are you a bad person or a person who acted badly?"
Judging behaviors and not people is a trait of rational thinking. Condemning the sin and not the sinner will produce fewer wrongdoings; damning the sinner will lead to making more mistakes. Distinguishing what one does from who one is better serves and maintains your mental health.

130. "When you act favorably, are you a good person or a person who has acted well?"
Like the previous question, this one leads into the value of rating performances and traits without judging people.

131. "When you act stupidly or foolishly, are you stupid or a fool, or are you a person who acted stupidly or foolishly?"
Dr. Albert Ellis, founder of Rational Emotive Behavior Therapy and grandfather of cognitive-behavior therapy, defined neurosis as "stupid behavior by a non-stupid person." What he was advocating was the abolishment of self-definitions. The most anti-mental health thing you can do is judge yourself. To repeatedly question clients' tendency to do so is perhaps the most important goal of therapy.

132. "How can you reprimand and alter your behavior without reprimanding or altering yourself?"
Supporting the idea of behavioral change without self-

blame comes through in this inquiry. Energy lost in self-blame can be reinvested in a plan to do better in the future rather than condemn self in the present.

133. "Do you think that there is a difference between trying to perfect something and trying to be perfect?"
Conscientiousness and craftsmanship are desirable goals that will instill much meaning into life's projects. Clients who insist that they be perfect at what they are perfecting will bring on head- and heartache. This question begins to make the important distinction between non-ego and ego pride. Wanting to do well in an effort to be better off is quite different from trying to be perfect so as to become a better person. Separating doing from doing perfectly well with clients allows them to approach important projects in their lives in a less stressed, more clearheaded way.

134. "Do you see any value in tallying and appreciating your strengths, advantages, and successes without esteeming or in any way judging yourself by them?"
Helping clients to itemize and to affirm their strengths, but steering them away from using any of these external props to esteem themselves, is a giant step in the emotionally healthier direction of unconditional self-acceptance. Teaching clients the how-to and the value of ripping up their personal accounting system, whereby they positively rate and esteem themselves for their good deeds, is a welcome addition to an emotionally healthier outlook.

135. "Do you think that there is a difference between practical dependency and emotional dependency?"
Show clients that although they are beholden to others for certain things, e.g., to their boss for signing their paychecks, they are not dependent on that same person for them to accept themselves or to enjoy their life. This permits them to free themselves to be more their own person. Comprehending the differences between these dependency ties results in emotional gains within gains;

this distinction can be made not only in the immediate situation, but in any problematic circumstance that is to be coped with for the rest of one's life. Practical dependence is a fact of our interdependent life; emotional dependency is a fiction that is not required, but is excess emotional baggage.

136. "Must people and events be the way you would like them to be?"
     Emotional sanity is to be preferentially motivated; emotional disturbance is to be demandingly insistent about one's goals and objectives. To drive home this distinction between preference and demand is a task that bears repeating. To give clients the opportunity to sort out want and demand does not guarantee emotional relief, but it is unlikely that you will get clients to give themselves emotional relief until they are able to draw this differential conclusion.

137. "Because something is good, does that mean that you have to have it?"
     The more graphically you can portray for clients the value of ceasing to become their own worst dictator, the more likely they will become their own best advisor. Nice and necessity are not like applesauce that runs together. It reduces the strain of going without to logically conclude that just because taffy or blue skies are good, it is not mandatory that one have them.

138. "Do you believe that, because something is bad, it must not happen to you?"
     If clients give indication of such a grandiose belief, a good follow-up question is "Where does that belief get you?" Until clients are able to admit to and for themselves the emotional and behavioral disadvantages of their faulty thoughts, they will be unlikely to work with you on developing healthier replacements of them.

139. "What do you think would be the advantages of focusing more on what you are doing rather than how well you are doing or what others might be thinking about what you are doing?"

Due to its paralyzing nature, clients need to be shown that it is advisable to avoid becoming a spectator at their own performances. This increases skill development. Due largely to overconcerns of others' potential disapproval, clients often focus on doing more of the right things and end up doing more of the wrong things. "Stage fright" responses can be controlled by rationally concluding that the world isn't a stage after all and consequently no one requires a good review from reviewers. From the less emotionally dependent standpoint, the client can begin to train him/herself to focus more on content and less on outcome.

140. "Granted that fear, anxiety, depression, and other such emotional states are unpleasant, how can you learn and what would be the advantages of learning how to be more tolerant and accepting of such discomforts while not startling or intimidating yourself by them?"
    Clients often further upset themselves about their original upsettedness by demanding immediate comfort. They can be taught to better contain their unwanted upsets by accepting them more to begin with. To strongly self-state "I shouldn't feel so anxious," "I must not be depressed," or "Feeling nervous is awful, I can't stand it" creates a multiplying effect whereby emotional flames are fanned rather than doused. Challenging thoughts that question "Where is the law of the universe that says I am in this world to feel comfortable on cue?" allow for an encountering of more helpful and healthy emotions. Years ago my children gave me a plaque for Christmas that read "Smile, dammit!" These words reflect humans' tendency to stress themselves about their symptoms, leading to problems about problems, rather than problem containment. This philosophic question begins to address symptom despisement as part of a more general human problem of demandingness and overreaction.

141. "Do you think that there is a difference between what is important and what is all-important?"

Clients often put all their eggs in a one goal basket. Consequently they unnerve themselves about the possibility of spilling the eggs–making it more likely that they will spill them. When clients are persuaded to see the importance of convincing themselves that if one part of their world is lost, the rest isn't required to go down the tubes, they can approach their goals in a more settled, well-thought-out manner.

142. "What do you think of the notion that you're not responsible for someone else's problems and disturbances?" Generating a sense of humility for what one person can do to and for another is a large piece of relationship problem solving. When clients are shown that they aren't capable of transplanting attitudes and feelings into another, they stop trying to do the impossible–saving someone from him/herself. Consequently less pressure is put on the relationship, increasing the likelihood of promoting more realistic, happier things in it. Additionally, acknowledging limitations as to what one can and can't do to and for another dissolves any guilt caused by the perfectionistic insistence of attempting the impossible task of trying to do someone else's work for him/her.

143. "What do you think is the value of being true to yourself as being more important than gaining another's approval?" To gain the comforts of another's short-run favoritism is a small gain when compared to the long-run losses that accrue from not being true to yourself. Self-confidence is lost from frantic efforts to gain others' approval because the individual thinks he cannot tolerate life, e.g., "I can't stand disapproval" or accept himself, e.g., "I'm nobody without the liking of others." Selling out on one's values to gain others' approval is an ill-advised trade-off, as it exhibits a compromising manner in which to approach life.

144. "Do you think that there is a difference between being influenced or affected by someone or something and making oneself disturbed by them or it?"

Humans are born affectable. They are affected or influenced by any life circumstances that occur within the context in which they live, e.g., within their family, political, economic, work, and ecological systems. These system occurrences have a bearing on human emotion. However, as much as an individual is affected by past or present life happenings, he/she cannot become disturbed by them. Only the demand for what people are affected by to not exist can cause disturbance. For instance, any person will be affected by harsh weather, e.g., extreme heat or cold, but only if people tell themselves that such ecological inconveniences should, must, ought not exist, e.g., "It shouldn't be so cold and it is awful that it is," will they create emotional disturbance. It is the demandingness and exaggeration that causes emotional disturbance, not the system happening. Or, a person who has been emotionally, physically, and/or sexually abused as a child is naturally going to be decidedly influenced by such occurrences. However, again it is the demand, exaggeration, and self- and/or other blame that will create disturbed emotions, e.g., anger, hurt, rage, fury, depression. It is the protest against reality, the exaggeration of it, the personalization factor, the self- and/or other blame for it—not the abuse itself—that will do the individual in emotionally, e.g., "This should not have happened, I can't stand the fact that it did, and what a bad person I am and/or my perpetrator is for being a part of this bad happening." To proclaim that one is affected or influenced by something is to say virtually nothing in that all of us are affected by exposure to whatever stimuli cross our path. To help clients make the distinction between influence and disturbance is to assist them in sorting out their emotions and not being afraid of what is found.

145. "What do you think about the idea that, because it took a long time to create a problem, it is going to take a long time to solve it?"

Much time can be saved by not literally buying into this self-fulfilling promise, e.g., if client and counselor take on this conspiracy it is likely they are perhaps unknowingly promising themselves to make it a reality. Better to instruct clients that it *might* take much time but *not* necessarily so. This is an encouraging question in that it leaves room for more immediate change. Faster-moving expectations make the therapy more invigorating for both client and therapist.

146. "What do you think is the difference between being yourself and proving yourself?"
Prodding clients toward an unconditional acceptance of self is a primary target of therapy and can be done by asking questions such as this one. To get clients to be themselves with their social group rather than desperately trying to prove themselves to their social group provides them with comforting emotional slack.

147. "What does the idea that 'nothing seems to work but working' mean for you?"
Clients who are reluctant to get out of their easy chair to answer the door when opportunity knocks can often benefit from heavy doses of the reality directly stated in this question.

148. "What do you think is meant by perspiration creates inspiration and not vice versa?"
Getting clients to work hard rather than to hardly work requires ongoing reflection on how the line of least resistance often turns out to be the line of most resistance. Clients are frequently content to wait for a mystical spirit to give them utterance, for the tomorrows that never seem to come. Taking the first step toward change whether one feels like it or not can be taught as a momentum builder that is made to start by getting started.

149. "Do you think that there is a distinction between wondering and worrying about something?"
It is important to clients that wonderment about what the future will bring creates a healthy sense of anticipation and participation while worrisomeness about it will cause anguish. Worry constitutes a concern that is preceded by "Wouldn't it be awful if . . . ." Emotional concern is

pyramided into emotional consumption, involvement escalated into entanglement by "awfulizing." When clients follow instructions and minimize the words "awful," "terrible," and "horrible" in their vocabulary, they are often quite pleased to discover that such a small semantic adjustment can be of large emotional benefit.

150. "Do you think that because up until now you haven't been able to succeed at something means that you couldn't ever do so?"
Everlasting thinking blocks possibilities. Clients are likely to try more often when they are shown that, though success has eluded their grasp thus far, if they continue to reach, opportunities can still be turned into accomplishments. Bending their thinking about the possibility of future success, rather than restricting it to the inevitability of past failure being repeated, converts into hope and effort.

151. "What does the idea that 'Those who run from pain suffer more, and those who face it suffer less,' mean for you?"
When clients avoid exposing themselves to their fears, they strengthen them. Building a strong case for a philosophy of non-avoidance and sustained effort is an ongoing therapeutic goal. "Present pain for future gain," that it is more painful in the long run to avoid rather than face the discomfort required to achieve a given result, is an insight that if acted upon will result in more pleasure and less pain over the course of a lifetime. This question begins to explore the advantages of cultivating a philosophy of long-range hedonism.

152. "What do you think might be the advantages of your developing the ability to give with no expectation of return?"
Happiness can be defined as a direct ratio between what you expect and what you get. To want but not demand a return on an interpersonal investment is a therapeutic proposal worth considering. Introducing clients to and persuading clients of the benefits of this philosophy of nonreciprocation helps them to lighten rather than tighten up when

their associates disappoint them. Expecting less prevents feelings of betrayal from building up a head of steam and disrupting more desirable feelings. The message is to hope for, wish for, and want a return on your provisions without demanding that you "need" such a return.

153.   "What is your thinking about the idea that because something bad has often been made to happen, like failure, that it has to continue to be made to happen?"
Overgeneralized thinking concludes that the present and the future will always turn out like the past. Seeking evidence for such a fatalistic perspective and finding none can be a beginning in coaxing clients to consider the possibility of more favorable outcomes. Until they permit themselves to envision less deterministic possibilities it is unlikely that they will determine to try to create them.

154.   "Do you think that there is a difference between being alone and being lonesome?"
Clients often present problems of going solo. Partly this is due to their own presumptuous idea that being alone naturally brings on loneliness. Teaching clients to not catastrophize about or put themselves down for being alone prevents a unification of being alone and being lonesome. This question opens up for discussion the anatomy of these two states, questioning the automatic sameness of them.

155.   "What do you think of the idea that your advantages make you better off but do not make you a better person; that your disadvantages make you worse off, but do not make you a worse person?"
This is another question that tries to avoid the rating game in which loftier judgments of self are given when able to control for the good things in life and lower self-definitions are given when not being able to do so. Clients frequently feel encouraged from learning the cognitive skills at their disposal to prevent the emotional seasickness that stems from the up-and-down rating of the self report-card game. Getting clients to see ego, self-estimations of various sizes, shapes, and forms as evil

and to be avoided is perhaps the most difficult yet most important outcome of therapy. Humans seem insistent upon judging themselves, e.g., proving their self-worth, increasing their self-esteem, heightening their self-concept, and deifying their self-image, and extra elbow grease on the part of the therapist is usually necessary to persuade them to do otherwise—to more fully accept themselves—*without* any external props.

156. "What is your opinion about the thought that anything you believe you can disbelieve?"
Highlighting clients' freedom of choice conveys their ability to empower themselves to control their feelings by their specific beliefs and more general philosophies of life. Preparing clients to assess and change their thinking can be done by calling to mind the fact that they are quite capable of doing so.

157. "How do you think the idea that 'Nothing in life has to be' fits into helping yourself to feel more the way you want to feel and less the way you don't want to feel?"
This single rational thought, when woven strongly and consistently into everyday thinking, has the potential to further emotional well-being perhaps like no other. The tripod of rational thought under the "nothing in life has to be" umbrella, "I don't have to be perfect," (and I'm not perfectly worthless when I'm not), "You don't have to treat me perfectly (and you're not perfectly worthless when you don't) and "Life doesn't have to be perfect (and it's not perfectly worthless when it isn't)" provides the cognitive tools that can interact with the emotive and behavioral components of the human experience to enhance that same experience.

158. "Do you see a difference between practical and emotional victimization?"
Demeaningness is a state of mind; no one can provide another with such a state. Others' harsh, cruel behavior toward us is a practical victimization of us in that it takes away our freedom of choice because we didn't ask to be

abusively selected against. Emotional victimization is self-created and comes from a self-putdown and is part of a more general problem of personalization. Making this distinction outlines hope for emotional sufficiency following even the most difficult of adversities.

159. "What would be some advantages to your not putting off until tomorrow what has already been put off until today?"
Building a case for anti-dillydallying, nonshirking behavior, against goofing or sidetracking, is a fundamental helping-process goal. Humans easily drift away from completing well-intended projects that would enhance their long-range happiness and survival. A primary responsibility of the helper is to repeatedly remind clients that their good intentions had best be ongoingly backed by the right methods, that to move forward with constructive action requires that their shoulders remain behind the wheel and that their noses continue to be attached to the therapeutic grindstone. Getting clients to itemize for you and to study and review for themselves the advantages of concerted effort will likely bring about increased problem-solving energy.

160. "Do you think that it is emotionally healthy to sort out the idea of sharing your life with someone from sacrificing your life for someone?"
Clients often can benefit from being taught that it is important for them to be concerned about the happiness of those that they love, but not at the expense of their own. They often feel emotional relief and get better interpersonal results from a more self-interested perspective that has them putting themselves first and significant others a close second, rather than others first and themselves a distant second. They are often grateful when they discover that, by being better to themselves, by sharing themselves and not sacrificing themselves for someone, they are also better for the other person. This is because they have fewer mood swings, are too active to be miserable, and therefore are more fun to be around.

161. "What does the idea that 'When you win an argument you frequently risk losing the relationship' mean for you?"

For most humans to be right constitutes "holier-than-thou-ism" while to be wrong comprises "unworthier-than-all-ism." Even when you think you are right, it is often important to keep still about it. When clients are taught to take the ego with all its sacredness out of being right rather than win the battle but lose the war, they more constructively lose the battle but win over the relationship. Pride is a bitter pill to swallow, but it strengthens the gut and relationship on the way down.

162. "What do you believe to be the difference between making a slip and creating a major setback?"

This question tries to introduce the idea that all is not lost following a mistake; it tries to disrupt the notion that the baby has to be thrown out with the bath water, that a bad situation automatically has to be made worse in the aftermath of an error. It is this domino theory, that if I push myself off the wagon of my good intentions I have to keep my foot on the gas pedal rather than apply it to the brakes, that worsens problems. Until this theory is put to rest, common mistakes will spread like wildfire. One mistake doesn't have to lead to another, e.g., one drink to two, one doughnut to two, one temper tantrum to another, one instance of procrastination to a next one. To encourage clients to have a relapse prevention method in place is to help them to cope better, to achieve to their fuller potential—to make mistakes but not to multiply them.

163. "What was this session like for you?"

Getting feedback from clients shows interest in and consideration of their views. Along with asking them what they learned, developing homework assignments with them, and your own summarizing perspective of the session, tuning in to their descriptive experience is one of the most appropriate ways to wind down a session.

164.   "Let's pretend that I believe like you, for instance, that I'm no good or that something is awful. How could you try to talk me out of these beliefs?"
Playing devil's advocate by pretending to take on clients' beliefs and suggesting that they try to convince you to believe otherwise can be quite revealing. The clients usually discover that they have some of their own best advice, but that it is easier to give than it is to follow. When the client is asked "What do you think life would be like if you followed your own suggestions?" he/she often sees advantages to such an endeavor. Getting clients past Alfred Adler's statement, "It is easier to fight for your ideals than it is to live up to them" or Mark Twain's observation "To be good is noble, to teach others to be good is more noble yet–and less of a hassle" can be done by assigning the homework of the clients to be to give themselves the same advice they would give to someone else in a similar difficult life circumstance.

165.   "What do you think of what I just said? My suggestion?"
Prompt follow-up to your suggestion better assures consideration of implementation of them. Advice will be glossed over unless consideration of its merit is sought. Leading with your hypothesis, active-directively going to the client can be especially helpful when you gain his/her opinion following your outreach. That way the client becomes an active sounding board of recommendations generated.

166.   "Would you like some suggestions?"
Unsolicited advice usually goes over like a lead balloon; getting the green light before eliciting your sage advice makes your suggestions more attractive. So, when clients are at a loss to express a better way to think or act differently about their old problems, ask if they would like some alternatives to consider *before* telling them what they are.

167.   "What do you remember most from the last session that was helpful?"
Starting where you left off, recalling helpful hints, is a practical way of connecting from one meeting to the

next. It can develop back into additional possibilities that will provide even better problem-solving services.

168. "What thoughts and behaviors did you notice that you did differently that were especially helpful since our last meeting?"
Begin by focusing on specific thoughts and deeds that bear repeating due to their helpful nature.This allows the session to commence on an upbeat note.

169. "Since we last met, can you name a thought or behavior that caused a setback for you that you would prefer not to repeat?"
Discovering 'how not to do it' can be as important as learning "how to do it." Identifying self-made booby traps helps to avoid future disadvantages. This process of elimination is a therapeutic task worth pursuing.

170. "Which do you think is more accurate: for you to say 'that's the way it happens' or 'that's the way I make it happen?'"
Humans prefer to see themselves as passive bystanders of, rather than active participants in, their own emotional disturbance. When clients see themselves as being active as their own worst enemy they often are better able to transpose this emotionally destructive energy to more helpful problem-solving vitality.

171. "Do you think it is more accurate to think that things 'always' go wrong or 'sometimes' go wrong; that they 'never' work out or that they 'sometimes' don't work out; that things happen a certain way 'every time' or that they do so more often than you would like?"
Humans tend to exaggerate, making difficult situations into dreadful ones. This flair for the insignificant can be tempered with a view that does not make disappointments out to be bigger than life. Anti-exaggerative suggestions are a major factor in setting boundaries on emotional upset.

172. "Do you think you can figure it out? Let's see if you can."
Self-discovery is preferable and to give clients the opportunity for it is important. You may not want to wait for-

ever for them to do so, but getting them to scan their own problem-solving tactics gets them involved on their own behalf as well as gives them a certified vote of confidence in their potential to help themselves.

173.   "What are your thoughts about the idea that, if something seems dangerous or threatening, you have to be unduly concerned about it by continuing to dwell on the possibility of its occurring?"
Steering clients away from possibilities being made into probabilities or inevitabilities is an ongoing part of the helping process. Due to magical-thinking tendencies, clients often believe that putting themselves on worrisome pins and needles will head off catastrophe. Once they learn and convince themselves that thinking *doesn't* make it so, they spend more time doing and less time stewing.

CONCLUSION

The right question at the right time invites, encourages, and tries to persuade clients to think, feel, and act in ways that will make it more convenient for them to derive more pleasure and less hassle from life. Rational inquiries help clients move beyond the self-suggested resistance that changing themselves is too much like work. Clients tend to drift, meander, be inattentive, and get off task and target, and the right question can begin to reverse this behavior by redirecting such antics. No matter what problem-solving school of thought you adhere to, information seeking about the client and his purpose in presenting him/herself is done via direct questioning. To get to know, understand, and help a client requires therapeutic dialogue. These questions, appropriately interjected, help create food for more helpful and healthful thought.

The kind of therapy that I practice, Rational Emotive Behavior Therapy (REBT), is a specialized form of Cognitive-Behavior Therapy (CBT), and was founded in 1955 by Albert Ellis, PhD, President of the Institute for Rational Emotive Therapy in New York City. Dr. Ellis pioneered CBT, persisted against odds on its behalf, and, because of his profound influence in its development, is considered to be the grandfather of CBT, which is practiced by thousands of mental health practitioners internationally. REBT attempts to humanistically and scientifically enhance more desirable feeling states. These questions are designed to create a climate of emotional uplift by creating a rational dialogue from which more constructive thoughts, feelings, and behaviors can be created. Try out some of these with your clients, get a data base, and conclude from your own experience with them which questions are more likely to work with a particular type of client, and when.

SECTION II.
RATIONAL REBUTTALS:
FIELDING CLIENT CURVE BALLS
WITH LESSER MARGIN FOR ERROR

A Cognitive-Behavior Guide
for More Efficiently Responding
to Difficult Questions and Statements
Frequently Posed by Clients

Introduction

This section attempts to illustrate tact and tactics for making the problem-solving interview process flow more smoothly. The therapist best not get bogged down in clients' methods of avoiding the issue of acceptance. This is a key dimension of client resistance—refusing to accept the reality that one is an imperfect person in an imperfect world, surrounded by imperfect people. Persuading clients to face the realities that "I'm not perfect," "Others don't have to treat me perfectly," and "Life doesn't have to be perfectly easy" form the foundation of Rational Emotive Behavior Therapy (REBT) as founded by Albert Ellis, PhD in 1955.

Typically in an active, direct, persuasive manner the REBT therapist attempts to teach clients how they can overcome their protest against reality, their refusal to accept what exists, and thereby minimize the effects of this tripod of emotional disturbance that places demanding, unrealistic expectations on self, others, and life. You would think that while being led into uncharted, more tolerant, rational waters clients would welcome with open arms ideas that have good potential to provide emotional relief. No siree! William Shakespeare said, "The whole world well knows, but nobody knows well." The whole world well knows that they don't have to be perfect, that others don't have to treat them perfectly, and that life doesn't have to make it easy for them to achieve their goals and accomplish their ends—yet, many are reluctant to know well. This tendency to look an emotional-control gift horse in the mouth is often highlighted in the resistance-to-change questions asked and the contrary statements made following solution proposal. These common progress-blocking questions and statements reflect clients' difficulties with their own hesitations and sidetracking. What these demotivating inquiries and procrastinating position statements commonly are, and examples of how they can be responded to in a way that extends the purpose of the helping session, will be identified.

Not that it is essential that you be as quick on your feet as a Philadelphia lawyer. But when your client throws you a curve ball, it can be helpful to have a wide range of response possibilities to draw from so that you don't strike out. But if you do strike out, you do! This text is not meant to perfectionistically imply that there is an ideal response to every tough client question/statement and that you have to find it. Rather, what is said is that though the perfect interview doesn't exist, you do, and that therefore there is room for your own creativity of response. Your problem-solving responses aren't required "to go by the book" or this book. It is hoped that narrative response possibilities identified by me will stimulate your thinking thus adding to your existing practice-theory by helping to field clients' murky questions and statements so that the most efficient paths in the problem-solving venture are taken. Sometimes it is helpful to piggyback off things that you already know that are stated in a different way. I suspect this is what part of this reading will accomplish.

ELEVEN IRRATIONAL IDEAS

You are not required to have a therapeutic retort on the tip of your tongue for every therapy condition. To avoid bringing perfectionistic tendencies to your efforts to meet and beat client resistances, minimize the following irrational ideas that you might hold coming into the therapy. Each will put a strain on the problem-solving process and a damper on desired change.

- "I must have all the answers all of the time when my client questions the relevance of my ideas for him or her."
- "When clients position themselves in a way that discloses their opposition to my ideas I must (over) explain myself so as to win them over to my way of thinking."
- "There is an absolute definite, right, precise thing to say at each crossroads in therapy and I must find it in each and every instance."
- "I must always appear strong and confident to my clients and the only way I can do this is to at least appear to be Johnny-on-the-spot."

- "I, not the client, must take full responsibility for achieving the consensus and agreement absolutely necessary for successful therapeutic outcome."
- "When my clients don't understand me or agree with me I must become unduly concerned about it or else it might appear that I am not interested in them."
- "It is highly significant for me that I gain necessary approval from all my clients, and how can I do that if I am not always capable of rightly responding to all their contrary questions and negative statements in each and every instance that they present them?"
- "It is easier to avoid challenging clients' difficult questions and statements than it is to counter them, usually by agreeing with rather than disputing them."
- "My clients have no right to challenge my authoritativeness and experience on the topic and instead must obediently comply with my directives."
- "Because up until now I have deemed myself inadequate for responding to certain types of questions relating to certain types of problems, I could never learn to be more efficient in such matters in the future."
- "When I start to think about saying the wrong thing in the throes of client side-steppings and resistances, I must keep catastrophically dwelling on the worst possible occurrence."

ELEVEN COUNTER-IDEAS

Each of these eleven irrational ideas can be countered with:

- "In an effort to neutralize my clients' resistances I hope to have some, if not many, of the answers to their questions. But, it is not an absolute necessity that I do so."
- "If I overexplain myself in the face of clients' doubtfulness, they will soon have me over a barrel."
- "Just as there is more than one way to look at things, so too are there varied guidelines, not recipes for responding to clients' tough questions and statements."

- "Perhaps modeling my own fallibility has more value than compulsively trying to appear strong and in control."
- "My clients and I have a *joint* responsibility for attempting to get the most out of therapy."
- "There is no universal psychotherapy rule that says my client always or ever has to agree with me or that I must unduly upset myself about our conflict of opinion."
- "Gaining my clients' approval is fine but if I focus on that I will likely lose sight of doing what would be better."
- "Overexplaining myself to my clients puts me in a dependent rather than in an interdependent relationship with them whereby I'm working for them, rather than we're working with each other."
- "If I just respond in ways that tickle my clients' ear, that might get them to like me, but will make it unlikely that they will learn anything from me."
- "Granted, up until now I haven't fared very well in managing my response to certain problem areas, but that doesn't mean that I can't learn from my mistakes and make fewer of them in the future."
- "Brooding about the possibility of putting my foot in my mouth will likely only unnerve me, making it more likely that I will fumble."

How to Handle
Troublesome Questions
and Statements

Each of the 164 listed difficult questions/statements frequently posed by clients is followed by a sampling of response possibilities from the therapist. Commentary about the implications of the question, i.e., the clients' motivation for asking it as it reflects the clients' belief system is included.

SEVENTEEN FACTORS TO CONSIDER WHEN FACED WITH DIFFICULT QUESTIONS/STATEMENTS

Problematic questions/statements voiced by clients are often characterized and motivated by one or more of the following factors:

1. *Low frustration tolerance* (LFT)—Appealing for an easier, surer, safer method of change is a tip-off of the holder's exaggerated view of the difficulty that is required to achieve a given result. The stronger the appeal, the lower the frustration tolerance and the higher the anguish. Pronouncements such as "it's too much to bear," "it's too risky," and "it's too much to tackle all at once" reflect resistance to change based on LFT.

2. *Ego anxiety/fear of failure*—When clients state "Wouldn't I be a failure," "What a fool that would make me," or "I would be to blame if something went wrong" they are defining themselves by the (rotten) fruits of their labor. This view of failure as shattering results in excuse making, denial, rationalization, and defensiveness, which serve as potent forces for blocking efforts to change.

3. *Indecisiveness*—When probabilities are not good enough replacements for certainties, clients will "reluctance" themselves out of the starting blocks of change. "How can I be sure that this is going to work?" "How do I know which decision is better?" "How do I know when I've considered all factors?" One of my clients stated after I asked him what his decision was going to be, "I'll give you a definite maybe."

4. *An exaggeration of the significance of things*—Dramatic views such as "Would that ever be a catastrophe!" "That would overwhelm me," and "It runs and ruins my life" display a flair for overreaction. Such cognitive explosiveness dampens personal development initiatives.

5. *Difficulty accepting the inevitable*—Hard work, discomfort, being slighted, and failure are but a few of the assurances of life. Notions such as "I can't accept that," "I won't admit I'm in error," and "Don't tell me it might not work out" indicate pills that are deemed too bitter to swallow.

6. *Grandiosity*—Reflections that imply anointed self-righteousness stray from self-responsibility realities. Statements such as "Because I've paid some dues it's time for me to get what I'm owed," "I should be the one who doesn't have to work so hard," and "I know my way is best and that is what everyone should agree with" give expression to this self-centered perspective.

7. *Self-pity*—"Woe is me-ism" is seen in the asking of impossible questions such as "Why me?" "What did I ever do to deserve this?", and "Why do bad things always have to happen to me?" When voiced in a whiny, nasal-nosed manner they provide a heavier reading of this self-sorry emotion.

8. *Insecurity*—Lacking confidence in self brings on a flood of worry and anxiety. Statements that move away from rather than toward goal setting include "I could never do that," "I can't bring myself to do something so different," and "My knees would just be shaking too much on such foreign soil."

9. *A quest and demand for certainty*—"Once I know for sure," "I must know for sure," and "I need to know exactly what is

going to happen" are all commands that insist upon guarantees before plowing ahead.

10. *Complaints about not knowing tomorrow's answers today—*"Assure me of a rose garden tomorrow because without such pacification I couldn't make it through today" is the cry of the person who insists on the ability to look and predict ahead of him/herself.

11. *All-or-nothing thinking—*"This way or that," "something is either right or wrong," "good or bad," "either I'm capable or I'm not," "life will improve or it won't," and "I will either feel happy or depressed" are examples of this way or that-type reasoning. The implication of such rigid alternatives is that "you, my counselor, must explain to me what side of the fence this dimension to my life under consideration is going to fall on."

12. *Overgeneralization—*Something bad labeled as "awful," "terrible," or "horrible"; defining something as good and then insisting that because it is to your advantage you absolutely have to have it; and thinking of the possibility of failing and then rating yourself as a "failure" in the event of same, illustrate overstepping the bounds of the original premise.

13. *Disapproval anxiety—*Hesitation that reflects overconcern about what others might think is seen in the statements "It all sounds good—but what will others think?" "I can't disappoint him/her," and "I couldn't stand it if they didn't like what I did."

14. *Discomfort anxiety—*"But I would feel too nervous," "I would feel like a phony," and "I would feel so out of character" reflect demotivation based on fear of one's own discomfort while goal seeking.

15. *Conflict anxiety—*"Whatever you do, don't rock the boat," "I'm too afraid that I might ruffle someone's feathers," and "I couldn't stand it if I disagreed and got his/her dander up" equal the philosophy of avoiding conflict at all costs.

16. *Humor deficiencies—*Emotional disturbance stems from refusing to accept grim realities while taking oneself too seriously in relationship to them. Statements such as "There's nothing funny about this," "I dare not laugh," "This is no

laughing matter," and "Nobody better think this is funny" reflect an overly grim approach to life's hassles, too numerous to mention.

17. *Demandingness*—Perhaps the common motivational denominator that lies behind difficult questions/statements posed by clients is the tripod of cognitive and emotive insistances:

(a) "I have to be perfect (or else I'm perfectly worthless)."

(b) "You have to treat me perfectly (or else you're perfectly worthless)."

(c) "Life has to be perfectly easy (or else it's perfectly worthless)."

Rational Emotive Behavior Therapy tries to identify and change these three basic demands of the human condition as they are reflected in the variations of difficult inquiries and position statements made by clients.

TYPICAL TROUBLESOME SCENARIOS

Now that we have identified the motivational background for these hard-to-manage question-and-statement curve balls, let's begin to identify what they are, and some of the irrational ideas behind them, while including suggested rational tact and tactics for directly and forthrightly responding to them in a way that does not disrupt the problem-solving process. Confrontation, persuasion, and vigorous disputation are key words in efforts to extend, rather than derail, therapeutic ambitions. Therapeutic objectives include confronting the clients about their efforts to get themselves off the responsibility-for-self hook; actively-directively persuading them to take on a philosophy of admittance and sustained effort; and assigning them vigorous disputation tasks of a cognitive, emotive, and behavioral nature that encourage if not implore them not simply to have "insight" into their avoidances, but to forcefully and repeatedly do something to unblock themselves from such hesitations. The suggested helper's response to seeming-change boycott and blockage are by no means the "right" or "only" manner of fielding clients' impromptu resistant two-step questioning and commentary, but are alternative means of doing so that will supplement methods you already use. Mark Twain said, "It takes me three weeks to prepare for an impromptu speech." This text is designed to help clinicians better prepare for the moment of reckoning when their client begins to confuse the self-development issue with seemingly bewildering, side-tracking questions and comments. Samples of these questions and statements followed by commentary and suggestions appear below.

1. "But I don't feel like it."
    Waiting for an alleged spirit to provide utterance can be a long wait. To wait on inspiration to the neglect of the perspiration that produces it results in marking time. This comfort-trap inkling provides a convenient rationalization for inaction. "Blending in with the woodwork," "cocooning," and "not coming out of the womb" are descriptions for this avoidant position and the unusual, peculiar sense of comfort that comes from deciding to put effort on hold. The trick is to force oneself to the task, and whether one feels like it is beside the point. Whether it be assertively saying "no," speaking out in a group, or seeking a promotion, the feelings of nervousness, strangeness, queasiness, and awkwardness that often accompany change can be taken with you. Developing a philosophy of discomfort that is compatible with mental health so as to better acclimate oneself to these personal development growing pains is the major surgery solution to "I-don't-feel-like-it-itis." Engaging in tasks associated with unpleasant feelings can be done "as if" one felt like doing so rather than halting on the brink of attempted completion until one magically gets up on the right side of the bed.
        Getting the client to acknowledge his irrational ideas, such as "I must feel comfortable," "There must be a more becoming time and way to go about this," "I can only do things when I'm in the mood," and "Feeling out of sorts about this matter is just too much to bear," while offering the following alternative responses in an effort to get the client to think, feel, and act himself past his self-imposed invisible straitjacket, is suggested. Because their reluctances are part of a more general problem of

demandingness, as clients are able to get themselves past this stalemate they can transfer their knowledge to removing future self-created barriers.

- "What would be the advantages of trying whether you feel like it or not?"
- "Are you willing to do it even though you do not feel like it at first?"
- "Can you think of a time when you didn't feel like doing something for the first time that was good for you, but you did it anyway?" Follow up: "What was it like the second time, third, tenth time—did you feel more like doing it as you went along?"
- "How long do you think it would take until you feel like doing it?" Follow up: "Are you willing to wait that long?"
- "How will your life be better if you act against your feelings and how will it be worse if you don't?"
- "What would it take to disprove your theory that you can't possibly do something unless you feel like doing it?"
- "What do you think is the secret of some people being able to do things for themselves, whether they feel like it or not?"
- "What advice would you give an associate who said they couldn't do something until they felt like it?"

2. "Do you think this is fair and just to me?"
    Coming to terms with a philosophy of fairness and justice that provides service to emotional well-being is not an easy task. However, in that a flawed philosophy of these two ideals is at the root of much emotional disturbance, it is a worthwhile search. Irrational notions such as "The world and people in it must be fair and just to me (especially if I am fair and just to them)" lie at the basis of emotional upset that occurs when this command is inevitably not followed. Getting clients to better see that it takes a long time to discover something that doesn't exist avoids the wishful thinking that motivates the dead-end search for these two elusive favoritisms. Encouraging clients to rethink their dictates for eminent justice, and at the same time to stop looking in haystacks for fair and

just needles that don't exist, can be done with the following alternative responses:

- "Is there evidence that there is such an animal as fairness?"
- "What do you think is a good way of looking at a life circumstance that you believe is not fair?"
- "Let's say it isn't fair, what would be the advantages of accepting that grim fact?" Follow up: "Are you interested in seeking those advantages?"
- "Let's say this matter is unfair. Why must it not be so?"
- "What do you think of the ideas that everything that exists in life must exist because it does and everything that doesn't exist in life must not because it doesn't?" Follow up: "How might you apply these ideas to your experiences with unfairness and injustice?"
- "Would you be willing to try for one week to lessen the thoughts 'It must be fair and I must make it so when it isn't,' and decide for yourself whether you feel more the way you want to feel and less the way you don't want to feel?"

3. "I don't deserve this."

   This companion to question 2 fails to accept that we get what we got from life, not what we deserve. Getting what one wants and getting what one deserves are two different things. In fact the closer one gets to linking wants and defined deservingness the more tarnished the goal becomes. Clients are often amused when asked if they would always want to get what they deserved and that it might prove helpful to consider being glad rather than feeling self-pity or hurt when life doesn't respond to them in an allegedly deserving way. They often are able to see the implied folly behind their quest for deservingness—that, true, they want to get what they deserve, but only when it is to their advantage. You can meet and beat this summons for deservingness with these optional responses:

- "What would life be like if you always or even often got what you deserved?"

- "After glancing at the front page of the newspaper what might your views be on the topic of deservingness?"
- "If one hundred people didn't get what they thought they deserved, would all respond the same?" Follow up: "What would be examples of the differing wise and unwise ways some might respond?" Follow up: "Which of these ways do you think would be a better response for you?"
- "Can it be proven that you must get what you deserve?"
- "How do you really feel when you insist on deservingness?" Follow up: "Do you want to continue to feel this way?" Follow up: "What thoughts are in the unwanted feelings that you identified?" Follow up: "What would be a better way to think in instances of deservingness shortfalls?" Follow up: "Why would it be a better way to think? Convince me."
- "Do you think there is a connection between how a person thinks and how he/she feels?" Follow up: "Would you explain in your own words that connection and how it applies to you?"
- "People often demand deservingness. Oftentimes that demand comes in the form of a 'must,' 'should,' 'have to,' 'got to,' or 'ought to'—do you have one of these demands in this instance?" Follow up: "What would be a better, more permissive way to think?"

4. "Should I or shouldn't I—what should I do?"
    Humans search for recipes with guaranteed outcomes. These questions imply a demand for certainty and surety by way of "a" if not "the" right answer as seen in the irrational notions that "there must be a right answer and I must know it prior to my decision (or else I'll wait until hell freezes over to eventually discover it)." The demanders of prior knowledge fail to realize that there are no right or wrong answers, only answers based on present evidence. They often begin to sense the folly behind these commands when told that rather than upset themselves about not knowing for sure, they can be glad they don't know tomorrow's answers today because if they did they would be bored silly! This infantile cry for certain direction from the therapist as final authority can be

countered in ways that suggest that clients both question the notion of absolute correctness as well as their perceived inability to think for themselves. The "should" implies that there is a universal law that the client must follow in deciding. This frenzied insistence can be revealed and disputed with these following alternative responses:

- "I could tell you what to do, but that would not help you to become a better problem-solver."
- "If I told you what to do, would you do it?"
- "What are the range of possibilities that you have to draw from?"
- "What do you think of the idea that there are no right or wrong answers, only ones based on present evidence?"
- "A 'should' ordinarily means an absolute answer, meaning there is only one possibility; how does this black-or-white way of thinking cause you to feel as you approach your choices?"
- "What does the idea that it's not so much which decision a person makes but the state of mind with which they make it that's important, mean for you?" Follow up: "What state of mind do you put yourself in with that 'should'?" Follow up: "What would be a better word to use than 'should'?"
- "What do you think of the idea that sometimes it's making a decision that's more important than the decision itself?" Follow up: "Does that idea apply here?"

    5.   "I can't make a decision because I don't know if it is the right one."
       Similar to question 4, this statement reflects a dire need for successful decision-making outcomes and can be challenged by the following questions:

- "What are your thoughts on the idea that you cannot not make a decision?" Follow up: "How does this idea fit your decision-making dilemma?"
- "Would it be catastrophic if the results of it turned out to be negative?" Follow up: "Why wouldn't it be?" "Convince me that it wouldn't."

- "If your decision turned out to your near worst disadvantage, how could you creatively cope with such inconvenience?"
- "If your decision had negative effects would that tell you anything about you—would you be a bad person or simply a person who in hindsight made a bad decision?" Follow up: "If you believed *and* convinced yourself of the latter, what influence might that have on ability to proceed with making a choice?"
- "What would your decision-making life be like if you forcefully and repeatedly told yourself, my choices don't have to be the right ones, and when they regrettably and inevitably aren't, I can challenge myself to cope with the negative fallout of them without putting myself down for making such a disappointing choice?"

6. "Wouldn't most people feel angry if they were me—wouldn't you?"

   What most people would do in many situations is nothing to brag about. True, most people overreact to and personalize disappointment, making such responses normal. However, normal simply identifies on a bell-shaped curve the most typical manner of dealing with a particular circumstance—but normal is a far cry from healthy. Eating hamburgers and fries from a fast food restaurant is normal in that most people do so, but such eating habits by the majority are not healthy. What is the human thing to do—to overreact to and to personalize experiences—is by the same token inhumane in that you end up hurting a human being, yourself. In REBT we go out of our way to encourage rational nonconformity, to deal with life's events healthfully, however unorthodox and abnormal such actions might seem. Responses meant to bring out a therapeutic reflection on doing what is better rather than what is popular include:

- "Do you want to do what can be done to spite the other or do what is better for you?"
- "Do you want to live your life the way that most people do or in a way that is more beneficial for you?"

- "You could take your cue from how most people would cope with this matter, but how would that help you to learn how to better think for yourself?"
- "What would be some advantages of drawing your own conclusions on the best way to deal with this matter, rather than dependently letting the majority decide?"
- "What do you think Thoreau meant when he said that each person in his social group represents a majority of one?"
- "What do most people's choices, including your noble therapist's, have to do with what choice would be best for you?"
- "Do you want to feel better right now by conveniently addressing your decision according to others' perspectives, or do you want to feel better for the rest of your life by inconveniently taking the time and energy to develop your own philosophy about this sort of adversity?"
- "What does the idea that 'what is right isn't always popular, and what is popular isn't always right' mean for you?"

7. "But it's so easy to get angry."
    It is *not* easy to take the easy way out. This comfort-trap misconception that maintains that it is easy to take the easy way out can be prevented from being sprung by some of the following rebuttals that set forth and encourage a view that carries beyond immediate convenience to long-range fallout.

- "What do you think are some reasons why it might be hard to take the easy way out by way of anger expression?"
- "Why do you think anger, though easy to express, has difficult fallout consequences?"
- "What do you think are the most difficult consequences of 'easily' making yourself angry?" Follow up: "Do you think that those difficult consequences are worth you 'easily' making yourself angry?"
- "If anger is so easy to express, how come it makes life so difficult?"
- "When you say it is so easy to get yourself angry, do you mean in the long run or short run?"

- "If anger practically always begets anger, how can it be so easy to vent?"
- "Anger comes from a demand; do such dictates really make life easier?"
- "What does this idea mean for you: 'As easy as it is to get yourself angry, it's easier not to'?"
- "What does this idea mean for you: 'As hard as it is to restrain anger, it's harder not to'?"

8. "Sounds good, but it's easier said than done."
   Granted, it is easier to make a talking decision than a doing decision and just because a plan looks good on paper doesn't guarantee its success, but a person would do well to start someplace. A line of questioning that steers the client away from making excuses for inaction had best be called into play. By his/her statement the client may be setting him/herself up to halt upon the brink of change, overfocusing on the difficulty required to go through beyond the planning stage. Questions and comments that invite and encourage follow-through rather than a derailment of goals include:

- "How many activities can you name that are good for you that are easy to do?"
- "What is so hard to do that hasn't been done before?"
- "Is it the load that's more difficult, or your thinking about the load?"
- "What does it mean for you that a goal is 'easier said than done'?"
- "How does it follow that just because something is easier said than done, that it can't be done?"
- "What do you think of staying with the idea that 'doing gets it done,' rather than concentrating so much on how much harder it is to do than it is to say?"
- "Why would this project really be easier done than said in the long run?"
- "What would be the advantages of switching your thinking from 'easier said than done' to 'better done than said'?"

9. "Why won't things work out for me?"
    Oftentimes matters of life don't come together for un-specified rather than for special reasons. Often clients insist upon answers to questions that are unanswerable. Given this turbulent request it would be important for the therapist to not go off course by looking for answers as if they were needles in haystacks. Such random searching causes paralysis of the analysis in the form of frustration that stems from trying to find something that doesn't exist. In a general sense things aren't made to work out because the individual either does more of the wrong things and fewer of the right things or does more of the right things but finds that one of the wrong things out-weighs many or even all of the right things by way of life impact. On the other hand, a person can do many or all of the right things and get poor results or many or all of the wrong things and get good results. Life's incongruities, all of those things too numerous to mention that don't add up, can be made to confuse matters further if the therapist lets herself get taken in by the client's impossi-ble search. This futile uncovering effort can be avoided by leading with some of the following position state-ments and questions:

- "Do you believe that there must be special and specific rea-sons why accidents sometimes happen in even the best regu-lated of life circumstances?" Possible follow-up question: "Where is the evidence that this is so?"
- "What do you think of the idea that we live in a random, im-partial world and that therefore things happen simply because the conditions of life randomly come together to produce the happening?"
- "What would your problem-solving life be like if you took pressure off yourself by stopping insisting that you find rea-sons of the universe for why bad things happen and instead put more focus on what you can do to better cope with them?"
- "Instead of concentrating on 'why' bad things happen to you or 'why' you or others do certain things, what do you think of

instead studying 'what'—what can I do to help myself to cope—
and what are the consequences of my efforts so that I can learn
from examining them?"

- "Sometimes when people ask 'why won't things work out for
  me' it is because they feel hurt and/or self-pity. Does this fit
  for you?" Follow up: "Do you want to learn how to feel less
  hurt and/or self-pity?"
- "Is it more that you don't understand why things sometimes
  don't work out for you or is it that you are having difficulty
  accepting what you know?"
- "Do you think that there is any truth to the idea that for the
  most part, we do not know, and never will know, why things
  happen in life as they do?"
- "Do you ever think that the universe owes you special explanations for negative occurrences in your life?"
- "How do you think you would feel if you consistently told
  yourself, 'The universe does not have to put itself on trial and
  single me out by providing me with favors by way of explaining why bad things happen to a decent-acting person like myself'?"

10. "It all sounds so simple."
     Understanding emotional disturbance is simple; correct-
     ing it is not easy. If this distinction between simple and
     easy knowledge and action, what you know, and what
     you do with what you know is not made, clients are likely
     to be disappointed when simple "insight" does not easily
     lead to better results. Disputing the simple = easy equa-
     tion in the service of more realistic outcome expectations
     can be done via some of these questions and comments:

- "It is simple, but simple understanding doesn't mean easily
  lived."
- "What things sound like and what they are, often are two different things."
- "Do you think that there is a difference between understanding and application?"

- "What were some instances in your life that sounded simple, but when it came right down to it you discovered that they were not easy?"
- "What do you think is a good way to approach something that appears simple from afar, but as you get closer you realize it's not easy?"
- "What is a good way to view something that turns out to be simple but not easy?"
- "How difficult do you think you will make it on yourself when you discover that there is such a big gap between knowledge and action?"
- "Why is it, do you think, that some people have an easier time accepting the reality that knowing and doing are often strange bedfellows?"

11. "I can't do it."
     This often-heard statement is the standard response for rationalizing inaction. After all, if I determine that I can't do something I don't even or ever have to bother to try. Unless this notion is contrasted with "I won't do it," clients will not get themselves out of the starting blocks to move toward change. "Can't" results in being beaten before you start, as it refers to action that you are incapable of taking; "won't" means that you have made a decision out of stubbornness to not do something that you are able to do but have simply dug in your heels and have refused to do. "Won't" allows for flexibility in that if you have made a decision to not do something you can put such a choice in reverse if you decide that it is in your best interest to do so. "Can't" has a whiny flavor to it, "won't" a bullheaded one. A near unexplained sense of peculiar, unusual comfort is garnered from determining that you had best stay in the dugout rather than compete for the impossible goal that you "can't" achieve. Getting clients to motivate themselves past this laid-back, give-up-before-you-start "can't" position requires understanding and forced, prompt action as reflected in the following countering thoughts and questions:

- "What do you think is meant by 'the person who says he/she can't do something is often passed by someone who is doing it'?"
- "If I put a gun to your head and threatened to pull the trigger if you didn't do it, could you do it then?"
- "What are some feats you have accomplished in your life that you originally believed you couldn't?"
- "What are some of the negative consequences you will experience if you don't get done what you say that you 'can't' do?"
- "Thomas Edison failed to invent the light bulb after hundreds of attempts. How do you think he prevented himself from saying, 'I can't do it'?"
- "Would you be willing to go for one week repeatedly telling yourself 'maybe I can if I try'?"
- "Are you willing to put your 'I can't' theory to an acid test by agreeing to call someone you don't like and agree to patronize him/her, or penalize yourself in some other agreed-upon way, if next week comes and you haven't wholeheartedly attempted to do this project?"
- "Do you think words that you say to yourself can motivate or demotivate?" Follow up: "What are some motivational philosophies, thoughts that you could use to better motivate yourself?"
- "If your child came to you and said, 'I can't pass my math test,' would you advise him—'You're right, there isn't a snowball's chance in hell you can pass your math test'?"

12. "I can't help it."
    This variation of number 11 further promotes a philosophy of hopelessness and helplessness. Number 11, "I can't do it," convinces oneself that there is no use in trying to *start* to do something, while "I can't help it" implies that the client has wrongfully done something that isn't in his best interest but is unable to stop himself from *continuing* to do so. Low frustration tolerance (LFT) philosophies motivate both these types of passive resistances—the same hearse, with a different license plate. "I can't help it" reflects LFT notions that to cease doing what is against one's best interests would require just too much effort and that therefore it

would be best for the client to set himself down to rest. Furthermore, "I can't help it" declarations often tip off tendencies to pout, not only about the effort required to halt a self-defeating behavior set in motion, but what the client will be deprived of (required to go without) as he concentrates on changing his behavior. The helpless-thinking holder of this idea often gives off signals that "because I can't help myself, others must come along and rescue me." The trick is to persuade clients to opt for more self-reliant and less emotionally dependent philosophies that would allow them to save them from themselves. These childish, baby-me-or-else moans that practically always accompany "I can't help it" can be debated with some of these optional responses:

- "Can you give me examples of when you started to think 'I can't help it' but ended up helping yourself in spite of your original pessimism?"
- "When you catch yourself thinking 'I can't help it,' how about rephrasing that notion to 'it may prove difficult to reroute old habits but that doesn't mean I can't give it the old college try'?" Follow-up question: "What would be the advantages of this different view? What would your life be like if you started to take it on?"
- "I'm thinking that you have given yourself a bad case of I-can't-help-it-itis—what does that condition mean for you?"
- "How do you honestly feel when you tell yourself 'I can't help it'?" Follow-up question: "How do such feelings cause you to stop you from helping yourself?" Follow-up questions: "What would be a better way to think? Why?"
- "Are you sure that the situation you've convinced yourself you 'can't help' isn't actually one you might have accomplished at some other time?"
- "What are some more optimistic ways of viewing possibilities for your life?" Follow-up question: "Are you open for suggestions as to what some others might be?" Follow-up question: "Are you willing to try them out?"

13.   "It won't work anyway, I've already tried that."
      Pessimism has its advantages. If you can convince your-
      self that you have already given a hypothesis the acid
      test, there is no sense expending the energy (a) to be more
      certain that you have in fact fully tested out the sugges-
      tion, or (b) to see that if with practice it can't be made to
      work. Clients often wrongly assume that because your
      suggestion reminds them of recommendations that they
      have heard and tried before, they are one and the same.
      By overgeneralizing, immediate comfort is gained when
      a client excuses not putting out effort that has allegedly
      already been put out. One therapeutic task is to persuade
      the client that the present isn't the past; because success
      was not realized the last time around doesn't mean that it
      cannot be realized this time. Clients need to see that the
      best remedy for failures of the past is effort that may
      convenience success in the present. Challenge their over-
      estimation of what has actually been tried and the energy
      that has been put into it. Use these rational counters:

- "Fine-tune what I'm suggesting you try and see if there are differences from what you have heard and tried before."
- "What is your precise understanding of what I'm asking you to do?"
- "Would you be willing to become your own best scientist by testing this hypothesis, getting an updated data base, and if you fail again, telling me 'I told you so'?"
- "What does the idea that 'the most successful people in the world fail the most' mean for you and how does it apply to you?"
- "What do you think of the idea of rather than waiting for success to happen, it would be better to go ahead without it?"
- "What did you learn from previous attempts and failures that you can put to use to increase the chances for success presently?"
- "If at first you don't succeed, try and try again—are you willing to try again?"
- "What would be some advantages of trying again, whether you succeed or not?"

14. "I don't have to forgive them and I refuse to do so!"
Forgiveness is often viewed as too much to ask, benefits
to emotional well-being notwithstanding. As difficult as
forgiveness is to accomplish, it is even more difficult not
to do. Meeting and beating client's pigheaded refusal to
forgive another for trespassing on their seemingly sacred
values is a strong challenge. Unforgiveness and vindictiveness are burdens that many would like to do without.
Instead they allow their own false pride and hypersensi-
tivity to get in the way of unshackling themselves. This
statement starts out with an accurate position–true forgiveness is not an absolute, but the client who steadfastly
refuses to do something should first consider whether
such opposition will contribute to long-range advantages.
Bringing to clients' attention the value of forgiveness,
while getting past its blocks and obstacles, can be done
with the following rebuttals:

- "There are a lot of things that you don't have to do, like wear
shoes, but that doesn't mean that it wouldn't be better for you
to do them. What do you think about what I'm saying?"
- "You have a right of refusal, but just make sure that you don't
die with your rights on."
- "If you follow up with your strong intentions to not forgive,
how might you end up spiting yourself?"
- "If you could, by choice or chance, find the courage in your
head and heart to forgive, how would that be of benefit to
you?"
- "Why do you think some people can bring themselves to forgive and some have difficulty?"
- "What do you think are some of the ingredients of forgiveness?" "What is its anatomy?" "Dissect forgiveness for me."
- "If there were one hundred people who were maliciously
wronged, would all one hundred be unforgiving?" Follow-up
question: "What do you think would be the differences between those who forgave and those who didn't?"
- "Do you know someone who finds forgiveness to be a natural
part of their relationships with others?" Follow-up question:

"Would you be willing to seek them out to discover what makes them tick?"
- "When thoughts change, feelings change—what thoughts would enhance forgiveness?"
- "What do you think of people who forgive easily?"
- "Do you see forgiveness as strength or weakness?" "Asset or liability?" "Good or bad?"

15. "I could never forgive myself for having done such a thing."
    A favorite pastime of humans and perhaps their most anti-mental health activity is self-judgment. Because of this self-rating tendency, a primary ingredient of efficient psychotherapy is getting across to clients that compassion begins at home. When a line of questioning that suggests that clients give themselves more emotional slack is pursued, good things are more likely to happen in the problem-solving process. Confrontive, persuasive, yet encouraging therapist's responses that push for a reexamination of this unforgiving premise would include:

- "Would you encourage a friend to forgive him/herself for violating the same standard?" Follow-up question: "If so, how would you express to your friend your self-forgiveness recommendations?"
- "Never is a long time. Are you sure you want to commit yourself to such an unforgiving time span?"
- "If you would decide to forgive yourself, how would you go about it?"
- "If you would decide to forgive yourself, what would some of the advantages be and what would your life be like with those advantages in hand?" Follow up: "Would you like some of those advantages?"
- "What do you think are some of the differences between a person who chooses to forgive him/herself and one who doesn't?"
- "Think of someone you have known who has managed to forgive him/her. How do you think they managed to accomplish such a feat? What do you think motivated them?"

- "What do you think the world would be like if more people forgave themselves for their mistakes?"
- "What do you think of the idea that it's an arrogant view to desire to forgive others but to refuse to forgive yourself for being less than perfect?"

16.   "I have so many problems and feelings that I don't know where to begin to start dealing with them."
Oftentimes when clients appear for counseling services they bring with them an avalanche of practical problems and emotional disturbances. These can be quite overwhelming–if the helper allows them to be. Some structure, priority, and organization would be in order if the helping endeavor is to be constructively focused. In Rational Emotive Behavior Therapy the ABC model of emotional reeducation is used as a guide to bringing some method to the client's numerable difficulties. Suppose at point "A" (adversity or activating event) the client describes a number of negative events currently affecting her life and then further goes on to describe a host of "C's" (negative emotional consequences or feelings, e.g., anger, fear, depression, guilt, etc.) that she has about those events. Before plowing into the "B's" (beliefs, cognitive distortions that cause the emotional upsets), lest a scattered problem-solving approach be used, it would prove helpful to pare down some of the multiple "A's" and "C's" so that such prioritizing can help maintain the helping focus.
My premise is that without a firm grasp of a primary real life problem at "A," as well as a mainly designated disturbed feeling at "C," efforts at helping the client may begin to seem like applesauce, where matters of concern seem to run together, lacking distinctiveness and helping efficiency. Suggestive, probing inquiries and statements that are designed to highlight specifically the problematic circumstance and the primary feeling about the circumstances are listed below. Properly used, they enable a better understanding of what life situation and what emotional upset the client wants to target. Once the distinc-

tive "A" and "C"are in place you and the client can find out the "B's," beliefs–the philosophical origin of the emotional disturbance. Rational alternative responses to this cluttered statement are designed to give the helping process more distinctiveness and focus. These include:

- "It sounds as if you have a rather large number of life problems and a mixed number of emotional upsets about them. In getting at and solving the kinds of concerns you have it's usually better to do a lot of one thing rather than a little bit of a lot of things. What do you think about what I'm saying?"
- "Oftentimes, when the right problem-solving methods are concentrated on one problem, what is learned can be applied to solving other problems as well; this is what I call the domino theory of problem-solving."
- "Unless we have a road map as to specifically where we want to get to, we may never get there."
- "Rather than go down blind alleys by experimenting with preliminary, bits-and-pieces problem-solving, what do you think of the idea of getting choosy by jumping right into the main event and see if we can't save some time?"
- "Rather than put out fires here and there, would you be willing to examine what you believe to be your biggest problem situation and unwanted emotion?"
- "If we don't stand for something by way of working with one of your problems above the rest, I'm afraid that we will fall for anything."
- "Of all the practical and emotional problems you have listed, which 'A' and which 'C' would you like to start with?" Note: Do this preferably after you have graphically listed them in collaboration with the client. (I do this on the easel in my office or on a blank sheet of paper.)

17. "I don't have any problems (though others think that I do)."
    Will Rogers once said that he never met a man he didn't like. In nearly thirty years as a practicing psychotherapist, I never met a client who didn't like/want to achieve a goal. Oh sure, sometimes putting a finger on what it

might be was akin to squeezing juice out of a problem-solving turnip, but seek and you will likely find. The epitome of a client reluctant to establish a conventional goal was a fifteen-year-old young man I counseled with many years ago. When he took a seat in my office I tried to prompt his involvement by asking him, "Son, what is your understanding of why you are here today?" He quickly replied in no uncertain terms, "My understanding of why I'm here is to figure out a way so I don't have to come to see you again." Fortunately I got the resistant hint and used what I consider to be a primary rule in breaking through to a resistant client–don't take them as seriously as they are taking themselves.

With tongue in cheek I retorted, "I was wondering what a nice kid like you was doing in a place like this to begin with. If I were you I wouldn't want to come back to see my ugly face again either. What do you think of the idea of us giving some thought to what can be done so you aren't required to come back to see me?" From there we began to identify who it would be necessary for him to appease and what patronizing behavior he could display to demonstrate his desire not to return to therapy. My point is–when you start with an identifiable goal of the client, there is less for the client to resist. Attempt to squeeze out that initial objective when it seems you are drawing a blank. Gain client cooperation without initial motivation. Be a catalyst for behavioral change without psychological or personality restructuring in situations where the client maintains his denial of problems, yet sets goals that allow for better accommodation within himself and between himself and his social group. The following rational rebuttals can assist in accomplishing these objectives:

- "I understand and accept that you believe yourself to be problem free. What are some problems that others think you have?"
- "If you did have problems, what are some that you would be more likely to have?"

- "Considering the problems others believe you to have, how would it be to your advantage to convince them that you don't have the difficulties that they accuse you of having?"
- "What sorts of disadvantages will befall you if you don't consider making changes that others, who perhaps have some authority over you, wish you to make?"
- "Let me ask you directly, are you willing to take a look at problems others who have some leverage in your life think that you have?"
- "What advice would you give to important individuals in your life who had the same problems that others accuse you of having?"
- "If you did have the kind of problems that you are accused of having, what are some recommendations that you would give to yourself to solve them?"
- "What do you think of the idea that mental health is a lot like dental health in that everyone has a few cavities, and that therefore eleven out of ten people have emotional problems?"
- "Let's assume that you find some truth in the theory that eleven out of ten people have emotional problems, which ones might you have?"
- "If you would agree that not everyone hates you, this would mean that you have problems because if you didn't everyone would hate you."
- "Did you ever laugh at yourself for making and admitting that you made a mistake?" Follow up: "What was that like for you—how did you feel afterward?"
- "If a person had a problem, what would be some reasons why he/she might not admit it?"
- "When a person admits to a problem, do you think that reflects more weak insecurity or strong security in self?"
- "What opinions do you have about people who admit to their mistakes?"

18. "Maybe I will."
    Qualifying statements provide an easy out, away from the effort required to achieve a given result. The long-range complication is that it is not easy to take the easy

way out, it only seems like it is. On the other hand, once-over-lightly commitments such as "maybe I will," "I might," "I could," or "possibly I will" can be an initial glimmer of hope en route to personal change. Directing the "maybe" toward a broader commitment, away from using it as a justification for later stating "I only said maybe—I didn't say for sure that I would do it," is the ideal to shoot for. Inviting clients to go from qualifying to committing can be done with the following questions and statements:

- "Better watch that 'maybe'."
- "On a scale of 1 to 100, with 1 being low motivation and 100 being the highest level of ambition, where do you think the 'maybe I will' falls compared to a more definite 'I will'?"
- "What does that 'maybe' mean for you?"
- "When you set a goal and tell yourself 'maybe I will do it,' what would your past experience indicate is the likelihood of completing it?"
- "Is there a better way to state your initiative than 'maybe I will'?"
- "If one person says 'I will do it' and another states 'maybe I will do it,' which one do you think is more likely to follow through?"
- "What self-statement do you think is more helpful for the purpose of making yourself out to be a more active participant in striving for what you want, 'maybe I will' or 'I will'?" Follow-up question: "Why?"
- "Is there any reason for bringing in the 'maybe' prior to committing yourself to 'I will'?"

   19. "Does psychotherapy/counseling work?"
        This question often asked by consumers of mental health professional activities implies a more passive level of participation by clients. The notion that human service providers are going to do something for or to consumers more than *with* them is a common misconception. Challenge clients to understand and accept the reality of "ask not what your therapy can do for you, but rather what you

can do for your therapy"; therapeutic outcome is often directly related to the amount of energy put into helping oneself. These concepts can be conveyed to clients by using the following challenging counters:

- "Psychotherapy doesn't work for you, you work for it."
- "Good psychotherapy guarantees you an invitation and an opportunity to help yourself, but it doesn't guarantee success."
- "In and out of psychotherapy, nothing works but working."
- "Psychotherapy and genius are a lot alike, nine-tenths perspiration and one-tenth inspiration."
- "Psychotherapy and the world do owe you something, it's just that you are required to work very hard to get it."
- "When the opportunities in psychotherapy come knocking you still are required to push yourself out of your easy chair to answer the door."
- "Benefitting from psychotherapy often means ceasing to put off until tomorrow what has already been put off until today."
- "In psychotherapy, as in life generally, if you're waiting for something to turn up you would do well to start with your sleeves."

20. "Whose fault is it, who do you think is to blame?"
    To err is human; to blame is even more human. Finger-pointing, identifying the bad guy in a dispute, is often made to be an overwhelming priority. Rather than go from opposite sides of the table while fighting each other to the same side of the table to fight the problem, participants are usually more inclined to dig in their heels in familiar territory. This question can be an attempt to get the counselor to take sides in the dispute. It also fails to make the important distinction between fault and blame. Fault is I or you made a mistake; blame is believing the one who made the mistake must be condemned for making it. Instruct clients that finding faults in oneself is important, because if fault isn't established correction is unlikely to occur. Fault zeroes in on desired changes but change is less likely to occur if energy is wasted blaming self and/or others for faulting. Stay out of clients' who-is-

right-and-who-is-wrong bickerings, identify fault without blame, and encourage clients to join forces against a common enemy. The therapist can help attain these goals with the following directives:

- "What do you think of the idea of acknowledging accountability without condemnation for what one is accountable for?"
- "How about if we establish a goal of solving the problem rather than trying to figure out who was more right or more wrong in creating it?"
- "If I take sides on this matter it's likely you both would end up disapproving of my actions."
- "Would you both agree that you each contributed to the problem and have something to contribute to the solution?" Follow-up question: "What is it?"
- "Let's get after the problem rather than get after each other."
- "I would suggest that we reprimand behaviors that go against the grain of progress, without reprimanding people."
- "Correct faults without condemning people. Try saying to yourself—correction yes, condemnation no!"
- "Would you agree that the best remedy for the faults of the past is to create successful experiences in the present rather than trying to fix blame for the past?"
- "I support that it will be more helpful to individually identify your own mistakes and how you think you can correct them rather than building a case for the other's faults and corrections." Follow-up question: "What do you think about what I'm saying?"

21.   "He has no right to do that."
      Although most people would agree on the general principle of free will and another's right to be wrong, when it comes to specific instances in personal life this permissive outlook is often reversed. Liberalism is quickly changed to conservatism when the issue at hand hits close to home. Until clients more fully accept others' rights to be the way they are, they will remain angry when others trespass on what they think is "right." Introducing the notion that humans have a right to go in

the direction they choose can be a touchy topic. This is due to the human tendency to make one's values sacred. When "I wish he wouldn't do that" is replaced with "He must not do what I wish he wouldn't, and has no right to do so," a golden rule is proclaimed. People generally don't like to be reminded of their Godlike, self-centered tendencies. Prior to their therapy they haven't learned to appreciate taking the sacredness out of their values in order to provide themselves with much emotional relief. Introducing them to the dark, demanding side of their values while pointing them in a more enlightened, non-dictatorial, emotionally relieved direction can be instigated by introducing the following alternative modes of thought:

- "Do you believe in free will?" Follow-up question: "How about this person's free will?"
- "What do you think of the idea that it is undemocratic to insist that someone doesn't have a right to follow a chosen line of thought and behavior?"
- "How does the idea that others don't have a right to follow their values make you feel?"
- "If your goal were to get yourself less upset with someone who betrayed your values, what would be a good way to look at their contrary-to-your-way-of-thinking notions?"
- "Can you think of any advantages to giving consideration to accepting others' rights to their own intentions?"
- "How does your belief that others don't have a right to go against your grain affect your relationship with them?"
- "What is your goal in insisting that others have no right to trample on what you believe is right?"
- "Do you think there is a difference in how you feel when you tell yourself 'He has no right to do that and therefore must not' and 'I wish he wouldn't do that but that's his choice'?"
- "How important do you think it is for a person to have a decent respect for individual differences?"

22. "But I have to find a way to help him/her."
     Humans frequently have difficulty exercising a sense of

humility as to what they can and can't do for another. Compelling oneself to answer the bell for someone else's problems and disturbances has a wearing effect that stems from the mutual resentment and increased emotional dependency that reflects the futility of trying to do someone else's work for them. When clients are instructed that no one has ever invented a way to transplant a more rational belief into someone else's head or a more pleasant feeling into their gut, and they begin to convince themselves of those brands of human limitations, other people's problems—and what can realistically be done about them begin to be put in more realistic perspective. Getting the point across that no one has ever invented a way to save others from themselves can begin with some of the following provocative and challenging questions and comments:

- "What will the world ever do after you're gone?"
- " 'If you wear your fingers to the bone for others, you will likely end up with bony fingers.' What do you think this means?"
- "Do you think that there is a formula for saving others from themselves?"
- "What does 'Florence Nightingale-ism' mean for you?"
- "Would you agree that you're good, but not that good, in terms of possessing the skills and stamina to do the work of two people?"
- "When you jump into, and try to solve, a person's problems, aren't you really treating the person like an emotional cripple?"
- "Would you agree that it is an impossible mission to try to rescue individuals from their own mistakes?"
- "What has been your observation of the end result of attempting to take care of things for others that only they can take care of themselves?"
- "How do you think one would go about realistically identifying what one can and can't do for another person?"

- "Think of a time in your life when someone darted into your life and tried to traffic-direct you away from your problems and disturbances. What was that like for you?"

23. "I'm fair to him, why can't he be fair to me?"
    Apparently one hand frequently doesn't wash the other when it comes to the "golden mean" of relationship accommodation. "I'll scratch your back if you scratch mine" ideals often fall short in the face of more one-sided realities. Fairness is not elusive or scarce, but more to the point, is nonexistent. This matter can be tiptoed around with clients or it can be challenged directly. I think that honesty is practically always the best policy in exploring the issue of clients' demands for a fair return on their relationship investment. Leading with a philosophy of nonreciprocation—the ability to give with little expectation in return—can prove helpful in responding to this question. Explaining that there is no evidence to prove that because you attach yourself to, assist, be kind, or in some other way treat another justly, that they are mandated to return such goodwill begins the process of expecting less and being happier more. Deestablishing the "reverse golden rule"—that others must do fair onto you just as you do fair onto them—can be accomplished by use of some of the following responses:

- "Why must others be clones of your fairness to them?"
- "Granted, a return on your fairness venture would be nice, but is it really essential?"
- "How does it help you emotionally to insist on special reasons for your fairness not to boomerang?"
- "In the ideal world it would be nice if one hand washed the other, but unfortunately we live in a far less than ideal world."
- "Because he could be fair to you, doesn't prove that he 'should be'."
- "What would life be like for you if you learned to better tolerate and more accept your fairness going out the back door, but not returning through the front?"

- "If for the next week you thought in terms of 'Although I would like a fair return on my investment in others I don't absolutely have to have it,' would emotional dividends follow such an investment in thought?"

24. "What good will it do if I come in if the one with the problem refuses to come with me or comes along only because he/she believes he/she is being forced into doing so?" (Mate, child, supervisor, in-law, etc.)
    Clients are often pleasantly surprised to learn that people who attend therapy of their own free will can be taught skills so that they can better cope with and influence their reluctant associates who either refuse to attend or who attend per someone else's insistence. People who don't want to be influenced can be influenced. It is possible to initiate questions and statements that begin to pave the way for the alternative notion that while it is true nobody has ever invented a way to change another's personality, people can be influenced in the way they respond to us by how we respond to them. Often the person interested in help has more leverage and bargaining power than is thought in affecting the not-so-interested party. For instance, if what the interested party brings to the relationship is threatened to be withheld by him/her if the other doesn't make some changes, a more equitable distribution of resources can often be arranged. Or, if the willing partner can be taught to not overreact, not fight fire with fire apropos the absentee party's upsets and disturbances, a more tempered relationship climate can be effected. Sometimes one motivated associate simply making an appearance at a problem-solving session can alert the absentee partner that change is in the air and it would be best for him/her to make some behavioral adjustments lest some disadvantages befall him/her. Examples of good questions for one-party counseling designed to encourage change in both partners are:

- "What are some resources you bring to this relationship that your associate would stand to lose unless further appreciation for your wishes is gained?"
- "Rather than proceed with jawboning as business as usual, what do you think of the idea of standing up for yourself by ignoring your associate's unpleasantries?"
- "What do you think life would be like if when your associate casted, you learned not to go for the bait?"
- "Trouble trouble and you will be troubled but by learning to pay less heed to it you can better control your feelings."
- "When your associate isn't being fair to you, you can learn to be fairer to yourself."
- "You can learn to care less without becoming uncaring, to overreact less and to not throw gasoline on bad events."
- "What do you think of the idea that you can sometimes influence another more by what you don't do and that you can be taught what not to do?"
- "It might do you some good to learn how to use this difficult arrangement to work on your own mental health—what do you think of that possibility?"
- "If you would learn how to save your breath with this person, perhaps you could learn how to breathe easier— what does that idea mean for you?"

25. "My child/husband/wife needs help and I want you to change him/her."
    Oftentimes the helper is asked to do the dirty work—sell a significant other of the client's a used car they don't want, reason them out of something that they haven't been reasoned into. Like question 24, the record should be set straight as to what can indirectly be done to influence another person and the unlikelihood of directly changing him/her. Realistic rebuttals to this "fix him/her" request include:

- "Change often comes in the size and shape of 'my, how you have changed since I have changed.' What do you think is meant by that statement?"

- "What is your opinion of the belief that there are certain things that one can't do for another, that they can only do these things for themselves, such as change themselves?"
- "A very small percentage of people enjoy the challenge and excitement of changing themselves. Do you think your significant other is one of these very few?"
- "What do you think of the idea that 'nobody has ever invented a way to change another person, that people can only change themselves'?"
- "How does the idea that 'you can lead a person to water but you can't make him drink' apply to your request that I change the other?"
- "Rather than reaching for the impossible dream of making someone else over, would you be willing to try to learn how to become more tolerant and accepting of what you don't like in the other?" Follow-up question: "What do you think your relationship with this other person would be like if you did build a case for greater tolerance and acceptance of him/her?"
- "What does the notion of 'using someone else's antagonisms to work on your own mental health' mean for you?"
- "What are options more promising than my trying to sell your loved ones a used car that they don't like?"
- "What do you think Helen Keller meant when she said 'Mankind has not yet invented a way to remedy the worst of all evils—the apathy of a human being'?"

26. "How come *every time* I try it *never* works out?"
    Humans tend to pour it on thick when it comes to describing the degree of their problems and failures. It is important to identify but not exaggerate what one is up against by way of a track record in efforts to achieve long-range happiness. Otherwise, discouragement is likely to set in from a view that leaves the client with a snowball's chance in Haiti of doing better in the future. Countering everlasting ideas such as "always," "never," and "every time" inspire hopefulness rather than hopelessness and can be accomplished by using some of the following inquiries and comments:

- "Do you think that there is a difference in how a person feels when he says 'sometimes' or 'often' rather than 'every time' or 'never'?"
- "Is anything ever really 100 percent?"
- "What have you learned from your past failures that can be applied in the present so as to increase the chances that the present not end up to be the past?"
- "How do these unscientific, absolutistic notions help you to move from hopelessness to hopefulness?"
- "Would it be fair to say that telling yourself that things 'always' go wrong, 'never' work out, that 'every time' you try you fail may well be a more than slight exaggeration?" Follow-up: "Where does that exaggeration get you, how does it cause you to feel?" Follow-up question: "Can you think of a better way to view these matters of fault and failure?" Follow-up question: "What are some (or would you like some) suggestions?"
- "Do you think it's possible that you could take some pressure off yourself by trying to look more at the part of the bottle that might be full?"
- "Even if the degree of your failings were true, how does it follow that you would be required to continue to follow that pattern?"
- "What are your thoughts on the idea that because something has consistently, and in your words continually, happened, that it doesn't have to continue to indefinitely be made to occur?"
- "Do you agree when you hear others say that things 'always' go wrong and 'never' go right for them?" Follow-up: "How do you challenge others' everlasting descriptions or do you just sit there and let them get by with fanning the flames of their upsets?"

27. "Why don't I change. Why do I keep goofing up?"
     Paralysis of the analysis sets in by trying to find special reasons why humans give themselves problems. Personal responsibility for change is often put on the back burner while pursuing the seeming magic of insight. Beyond their general tendencies to personalize and exaggerate,

humans give themselves problems for no special reasons. When a dialogue of "it could be this" or "it could be that" is used, the search for nonexistent problem-causing pawns is futilely made to happen. Avoid allowing this search for awareness to become an end in itself, where insight overcomes ignorance but little else, by using some of the following retorts in the service of more direct, instructional problem solving. With this more-concrete-options alternative, consequential thinking replaces trying to find a needle in a haystack that may well not exist to begin with!

- "What do you think of the possibility of instead of trying to figure out the 'whys' of your behavior, to instead look at the 'whats'–*what* were the consequences of your decision to do what you did and do you wish to continue to create those consequences in the future?"
- "What is your view of the notion that we don't know why we do most things in life but we do know what happens as a result of our actions?"
- "If after your search you pinpoint what you think would be a 'why,' how would that be profitable in changing your behavior?"
- "I think that humans come into the world with 'upset-ability:' the ability to upset themselves regardless of what specialized circumstances they are exposed to. What do you think?"
- "Would you consider the idea that even if given perfect upbringing on a utopian island, humans would still give expression to their personalizations and overreactions–and that therefore there are no special 'whys' to their conduct?"
- "Do you agree at all with the thought that humans will upset themselves in any life circumstance that is less than perfect and are emotionally freer the split second they stop looking outside themselves for 'whys' to explain their problems and disturbances?"
- "I'm concerned that if we keep turning over haystacks in our search for needles we will confuse our problem-solution purpose."

- "Rolling up your sleeves and correcting your concerns may well get you further than trying to figure out how you made them to begin with."
- "Doing (taking action) usually works better than stewing (seeking the 'whys and wherefores') in getting on with one's life."

28. "What if I made a wrong choice and it didn't work out?" Indecisiveness is often motivated by the fear of failure and catastrophic thinking, e.g., "What a louse I would be and how devastated I would become if I took the wrong fork in the road." Unless clients are offered a different structure of self-acceptance and tolerance, e.g., "my failure would be lousy and disappointing but that does not make me a louse or the outcome a disaster," they will continue to halt themselves on the brink of defining their priorities. Making it convenient for them to go out on a limb where the fruit might be can be done by using some of these counters and commentaries:

- "What do you think Mark Twain meant when he said, 'My life has been full of devastation and disaster–most of which has never happened'?"
- "What good things could you still make happen, even in the aftermath of your disappointing choice?"
- "What are some valuable things that you have learned from some of your less than desirable choices of the past?"
- "Give me your thoughts on the statement: 'Life is for lessons and you often learn more from failure than from success.'"
- "Where does it get you to view failure to make the right decision as being bigger than life and the worst of all possible crimes?"
- "Do you think that failure can lead to a more well-rounded personality?"
- "What does the idea: 'The most successful people have likely made the wrong choices the most' mean for you?"
- "What is your response to the thought that you can't avoid making the wrong choice by not choosing, that instead you practically guarantee it?"

- "You can run but you can't hide from wrong choices—how does that grab you?"
- "What might be some good things that you could learn from making a disappointing choice, that you could use in determining future decisions?"

    29. "What do you expect me to do?"
        Getting clients to see that what they expect of themselves is more important than what you or others might expect of them is an important step in turning the corner toward self-responsibility. Encouraging clients to follow their own lead while playing down authoritarian expectations that they may have of you discourages blind adherence to others' ways of thinking. Bringing clients to the point of identifying for themselves their own self-expectations while encouraging self-reliant thinking can be accomplished by offering the following alternative trains of thought:

- "I could tell you what I would hope for you but that wouldn't help you to think more for yourself about what your responsibilities and ambitions are."
- "What do you think is more important, what someone else expects of you or what you expect of yourself?"
- "How important for you is what I might expect you to do?"
- "What does what I might expect of you mean for you?"
- "Do you see yourself as more, less, or about equally likely to do what I might expect you to do?"
- "What would your decision about how to handle what I might expect of you reveal about you?"
- "If what I or someone else expected of you was deemed to be unfair, how would you deal with such an imbalance?"
- "Your question leads me to believe that you might tend to depend on me to lead you through your problems. Is there any accuracy to my hunch?"

    30. "But that's not like me; I've been this way all of my life."
        Largely because clients feel "phony" and give themselves a low tolerance for the initial discomfort required to try something different, they hedge on experimenting

with a new piece of behavior. Until clients begin to accept the initial discomfort as the entry fee for testing new behavioral waters and to imagine themselves doing so, they will continue to have difficulty forging ahead in their personality development. Getting clients to change their thoughts and images in their heads and then to engage in forced action can be done with the following disputes and directives:

- "If you ate horse manure all your life, would you be required to continue to eat it?"
- "Aren't you here to try out different thoughts and behaviors that, up until now, have been foreign to you?"
- "Looking back, have there been other times in your life that you did something for the first time and felt out of sorts, phony?" Follow-up: "What did it feel like the second time, third time, twenty-fifth time . . .?"
- "Would such a change really not be you, or would it be you paying the price of discomfort for doing something different?"
- "What are some advantages for you in doing something different?"
- "What are some advantages for you in doing something that is 'not like you'?"
- "Are you more likely to learn from doing something that is in character or out of character?"
- "Do the present and future have to be like the past?"
- "Would it be worth it to push yourself beyond your current level of comfort?" Follow-up: "Why would it be worth it? Convince me."
- "Like children who time after time take the same path through the woods, not stopping to think that there might be a more amusing, enjoyable path to take—what might you miss out on by continuing with business as usual?"

31. "Why should I (always) have to give in?"
     Getting clients to see that although they don't ever "have to" give in, at times it may well be to their advantage to do so, can prompt clear-headedness from which compro-

mise proposals can begin to be considered. Ego pride, resentment, and bullheadedness prevent efforts to more accommodate individual differences. Understanding the long-range advantages of giving in without cursing the seeming one-sidedness of the act provides emotional relief. Teaching clients rational ideas that allow them to nonresentfully compromise in the short run often pays long-run dividends through increased tolerance within self and toward others. The following questions and comments will direct clients toward making choices that will be in their best interests:

- "Do you think that there is a difference between deciding to give in because you 'choose to' rather than because you 'have to'?"
- "What do you think of the idea that a person doesn't 'have to' do anything, including survive, but may want or desire to do so?"
- "How could you decide to do what you are going to do by way of giving in but do so nonresentfully?"
- "What are some reasons why it is sometimes, perhaps often, to your advantage to give in?"
- "What are some favorable results that you have seen in your own and in other relationships when someone has 'given in'?"
- "Do you see giving in as a sign of weakness or strength?"
- "You have a right not to give in. Do you see any dangers from exercising that right?"
- "Why must you not, should you not, give in to better accommodate your differences with another?"
- "How might giving in be an act of self-confidence and personal security rather than insecurity?"
- "What image is presented by a person who stubbornly digs in his/her heels and refuses to bend his/her thinking?"

32. "Tell me, how can I find out the real me—who am I?"
    This rather vague, unclear inquiry can be a cover-up to avoid change. After all, if I search for something that has already been found—myself—I will never find it over again and can forestall the hard work required to change my

thoughts and behaviors. *Un*confusion occurs when more definitive, clear-cut goals are identified such as the specific things one wishes to experience in the rest of one's life. Otherwise the client is likely to end up groping for a mystical identity that can be more clearly defined with specific real-life goals. Opting for reality rather than mysticism in goal setting can be done by using more straightforward declarations and questions such as:

- "When you say that you want to find out who you are, don't you really mean that you want to discover what you want to do with the rest of your life?"
- "Would it make sense to you to brainstorm all the things that you would like to touch, taste, smell, and experience in the time you have left rather than trying to figure out what is already said on your birth certificate?"
- "What do you think of the idea that it's better to light one candle than to curse the darkness and that it might be better to shed some light on specific attitude and behavioral changes that you wish to make rather than curse the darkness beyond your obvious identity?"
- "What is evident is the fact that you're you. What isn't as clear is what are some of the advantages you would like to hook into in your lifetime?"
- "Would you agree that searching for who you are is more likely to promote stewing while striving for what you wish to experience and accomplish in the limited time you have left will likely result in more doing?"
- "How does it profit people if they seek themselves but lose out on prioritizing those values they wish to act upon?"
- "After all that's said and done, there's usually more said than done. What do you say we talk less about you and do more about what things you want to make happen in your life?"
- "Often the closer one gets to a goal the more tarnished it becomes; seeking out 'who you are' when you have already been defined on your birth certificate may lead to duplication of effort."

33. "How can I get him to stop upsetting me?"
    Guiding clients toward a philosophy of admittance is an important prerequisite of problem solving. Due to human defensiveness, the idea that "I trip my own trigger" is a difficult proposition to accept. Other-blame seems more convenient than self-blame—the idea that no one is required to be blamed is rarely considered. Consistently emphasizing that emotions are not externally caused and that each individual is responsible for his/her emotions is a message worth repeating. Humans will upset themselves in any life circumstance that is less than perfect and are emotionally freer the split second they stop looking outside themselves to explain their upsets. Clients need help to get a foot in the door by taking more responsibility for their own feelings, while becoming unshackled from putting themselves at the emotional mercy of another. This can be directed by these comments and questions:

- "If he was disturbing you, how come everyone in that situation wouldn't experience disturbance?"
- "What does the idea that 'sticks and stones may break my bones but words will never harm me—unless I sharpen them up and stick them in myself' mean for you?"
- "How does it follow that, because he doesn't change his ways, you must continue to feel upset?"
- "Which is more accurate, for you to say and believe 'he is upsetting me' or 'I'm upsetting myself about him'?"
- "What does the idea of not going for another's irrational harassment bait mean for you?"
- "Where is the evidence that this person must change before you can feel better?"
- "What is your hunch as to what would become of your upset if you made yourself less emotionally dependent on this person?"
- "What would be a good way to think about this person's negative comments if your goal were to not make yourself his/her plaything?"

- "How might the belief 'My, how you have changed since I've changed' apply in your relationship with this person?"
- "What do you think Mohammed meant when he said 'Tell me a mountain has moved and I'll believe you; tell me a person has changed his character and I'll disbelieve'?"
- "What good things can you make happen in your life if this problematic-acting person continues to act badly in ways that apparently come naturally for him?"

34. "What if I put forth all this effort and it still doesn't work?"

   An often overlooked component of mental health is creating a philosophy of nonreciprocation: the ability to put forth effort without demanding a return on it. That is not to say that it is not healthy to wish, want, prefer, or hope for a return on your energy output–but the desire for a reasonable return is a far cry from an insistence upon one. Effort spent but not returned is not wasteful; to encourage clients to view their efforts in this manner is to encourage trying, learning not to give up, and a more confident belief in self.

   A client came to me with a presenting problem of verbal abuse from her husband. I taught her some assertiveness training skills to distance herself from his contrary comments. When she came back to see me the next week I asked, "Darlene, how did you make things go this past week?" She replied, "Well, Bill, I tried everything that you told me to do, and none of it worked–but I feel better." Her efforts showed that success following ambitious efforts is nice, but not necessary for the purpose of helping yourself. The irrational notion that "whenever I extend effort on behalf of my goals I absolutely must get a full return on my investment and it is simply intolerable when I don't" has a demanding, exaggerating flavor to it that discourages the effort required to achieve a desirable result. This faulty philosophy of effort can be challenged by these rational rebuttals:

- "Looking back on your life, have you learned more from success or failure?"
- "If you would end up going down a blind alley, how could that help you to find your way home?"
- "What are some advantages of trying and failing?"
- "What do you think of the idea that trying is habit forming, and it is a good habit to form at that?"
- "Would it be fair to say that the world wouldn't come to an end, turn to green cheese, or cease to spin on its axis if you strenuously tried and failed?"
- "What is the worst thing that could happen in the event you busted a gut trying and still came up short of your goal?" Follow-up question: "How could you adequately cope with such disappointment so as not to turn it into a disaster?"
- "You take a guess, what do you think would occur if you gave it your best shot and yet that wasn't enough?"
- "What do you think of the idea of continuing to try hard, but with less expectation in return?"
- "What do you think of the idea that happiness is a direct ratio between what you expect and what you get?"
- "Your implication is that if you tried hard and failed that would be 'awful' or 100 percent bad; where is the scientific evidence for this all-out position, and what good does it do to awfulize about possible failure?"

35. "But that is (too) hard to do."
     Humans are allergic to work, they often break out in hives when it is mentioned. They often demand a womb-like existence without hassle and difficulty. Defining a project as too hard limits the amount of energy one is willing to expend to reach it; "now I lay me down to rest" is made to be the convenient byword. Challenge the above qualifying statement to head excuse-making off at the pass with the following disputations:

- "What are you asking yourself to do that hasn't been done before?"
- "Forget about the 'but' and get off your butt."

- "Especially watch what is said after the word 'but' because that's what is often really meant."
- "Would you agree that many things in life that are good for us are hard to do?"
- "Little comes easy but trouble and hassle; better that you do what seems hard to avoid these near givens."
- "What do you think of the idea of taking the long easy, rather than the short hard way?"
- "Do you find some truth in the idea that as hard as some things are to do, they are harder not to do?"

36.   "How come I always get the short end of things?"
      Self-pity is one of the more difficult emotions for most to accept. Yet, until its disguises are unveiled, the potential problem-solver is unlikely to be awakened from his/her self-indulgent slumber caused by this woe-is-me feeling state. This overreactive perspective that produces under-reactive results comes in varying sizes and shapes such as in the question under consideration. Discouragement pro-duced from this absolutistic, forever-and-always conclu-sion can be avoided by direct, reflective questions and statements such as:

- "What leads you to believe that there are special reasons for whatever shortage of advantages you experience?"
- "Better that you watch the 'always.'"
- "What would be a good way to look at things those times that you actually are disadvantaged?"
- "How have you survived up until now when matters are not made to go your way?"
- "What are some things that you have done wrong that have contributed to those occasions of being shortchanged?"
- "What is an example of your correcting a mistake that was the result of learning from getting the wrong end of the stick?"
- "What do you think of the idea that, when you are unfairly discriminated against, this constitutes all the more reason to be fair to yourself by not making a bad situation worse?"

- "What have you noticed in other's successful emotional self-management when they have come up short by way of the world's and its people's favoritism?"
- "What do you think of the notion that it's par for the human-condition course to be treated unfairly much of the time?"

37. "Whose side are you on anyway?"
    Clients have rules for counseling and if you violate them you may be the first to know. Especially in relationship discussions, consumers are apt to talk back when you don't tickle their ear. They come to their therapy wanting direct information but often their requests contain a qualifier: "Be honest in your opinion about my problems–but say what I want to hear." Such a double standard can be dealt with forthrightly with some of the following inquiries, designed to promote a more collaborative partnership·

- "How does my disagreement with you equate with being against you?"
- "I'm on the side of those ideas we can formulate that contribute to your long-range happiness and survival."
- "The side I'm on is the side of the table you're sitting on, so that we can join forces to compete against the problem rather than against each other."
- "Let's say for the sake of discussion that I was aghast about your values; how could you not disturb yourself about that?"
- "Is your being upset about my disagreement part of a more general relationship problem you give yourself when others betray your values?"
- "Why can't we agree to disagree?"
- "How about us seeking a common enemy and debating that, rather than disputing each other?"
- "Do you think you will learn more from someone who contrasts your ideas or from one who patronizes them?"
- "Can you think of some reasons why it would not be good for us to agree on everything?"

- "If we agree on everything it would just be another day at the office, more of the same—and progress often stops with sameness."

38. "I tell people who try to help me what they want to hear."
    This oppositional declaration serves notice on the helper that she is being challenged to do the client's work for him. This antagonistic, somewhat passive attempt to wave a red flag in front of a bull should be left relatively uncontested. It is a realistic goal to acknowledge your understanding of this overly ingratiating pattern without trying to change it. Otherwise, you will be futilely trying to do for others what only they can do for themselves. Avoid entrapment by using some of the following rebuttals that create a distance between clients' subtle invitations to do their bidding for them and your inclination to try to save them from themselves:

- "Where has that gotten you?"
- "How does that help you to better help yourself?"
- "What do you think would happen if you started to say what you thought rather than what you think others want you to think?"
- "What does 'others dislike you for your ideas' mean for you?"
- "How well do you handle disapproval of your opinions?"
- "What are you telling yourself just before you tickle the ears of those who try to help you?"
- "How do you feel immediately after you tell others what you think they want to hear?"
- "Do your thoughts just before and your feelings just after you deceive those who are attempting to help you contribute to your long-range happiness?"
- "What do you think of the idea that such a strategy wins your personal battle with your helper but loses the war against overcoming your problems and disturbances?"
- "What does the possibility that such a tactic results in cutting off your nose to spite your face mean for you?"

39. "I'm confused, I don't know what to do."
    When clients confuse themselves they often hint that they
    want their counselor to unconfuse them and do their work
    for them by suggesting a correct choice. Approaching the
    client with some of the following direct, potentially eye-
    opening responses that are designed to put decision-mak-
    ing responsibilities back on the client can prove helpful:

- "It sounds not so much like you haven't made a decision, but
  rather that you have made one but haven't decided *when* you
  are going to carry it out."
- "If your life depended upon deciding in the next ten seconds,
  what would you decide?"
- "What do you think of making a decision while feeling uncertain, living with it, and perhaps learning from it?"
- "Would it be accurate to say that one of the main reasons
  you're confusing yourself is by insisting that you make the
  right choice, and that you know the right choice before you
  make it?"
- "Have you just not made a decision or have you made a decision but have failed, up until this point, to act upon it?"
- "Must you know what to do before you do something?"
- "Could you survive making a decision based on present evidence only to find out that your choice had negative results?"
  Follow-up comment: "Explain to me, if not convince me, how
  you could survive even in the midst of a decision gone astray."
- "What do you think is wise for a person to do, when they don't
  know what to do?"

40. "Why else would I be here if I didn't want to change?"
    Making an appearance, wanting to change, and commit-
    ment to change are three separate entities. Either or both
    of the first two often do not lead to the third. This is
    because talk and appearance are cheap whereas commit-
    ments are expensive by way of the time and energy prac-
    tically always required to stand behind them. Doing, not
    talking or appearing, gets projects done. Humans have
    strong tendencies to go in the direction they are headed
    and it is often helpful to remind clients of other motiva-

tions for seeking help that would be well for them to avoid, e.g., to talk about and to appear on behalf of their problems and concerns, without necessarily getting themselves to the doing portion. The following rational counters to what the client believes to be the obvious are designed to emphasize the value of fuller commitment to change while conveying the no-nonsense message that you are onto the fact that humans often do use words as substitutes for action.

- "I'll share with you some of my other possibilities if you will share with me some of yours."
- "On a scale of 1 to 100, with 1 being low motivation for change and 100 being high motivation, which number would you assign yourself?"
- "Sometimes, if not oftentimes, people appear because they want to prove that they are right and that the rest of the world is wrong."
- "More than occasionally people show up for an appointment because if they don't someone who has leverage over them may administer some hell to pay."
- "What is it about your life that will be made better with change? What's in it for you?"
- "What do you think is the difference between presenting yourself for change and standing behind what you present yourself for?"
- "What percentage of people have you met in your lifetime who have talked about change without ever getting around to actually changing?"
- "Do you tend toward making more talking or more doing decisions?"
- "Do you think it's more of a human tendency to preach a sermon with one's life or with one's lips?"
- "Let me play the devil's advocate by saying 'I don't think you have good reason to change.'"

41. "What sort of person would I be if I tried and failed?" Clients frequently trap themselves by their self-definitions. They view failure as shattering and envision them-

selves as being subhuman in the event of failure. Consequently, they put off trying and as a result guarantee failure. Will Rogers said, "It's great to be great–but it's even better to be human." Actively teaching the clients that they will not become subhuman due to their failures nor superhuman as a result of their successes frees them to try, and likely succeed, some of the time. Rational recourses to this otherwise effort-limiting question include:

- "A person who failed–but not a failure."
- "A person who believed in him/herself enough to go to bat for his/her own behalf."
- "A person who finds enough value in his/her existence to come out of the dugout and get into the game."
- "A person who likely learned something from failure that can be applied to possible success later on."
- "A person who didn't wait for success, but instead went ahead without it."
- "How do you regard other people, especially those that you admire and respect, when they try and fail?"
- "What did it make Thomas Edison when, after 600 failed attempts, he put together the right formula to invent the light bulb?"
- "What do you think is meant by 'the most successful people in the world fail the most'?"
- "Are people their successes and failures, or do they make their successes and failures?"

42. "I think its all my fault, that I'm to blame. Don't you agree?"
   Clients often expect to be blamed, just as they frequently blame themselves. This question invites you to be part of the blaming process, but when answered correctly it can be an encouragement to the client to give himself/herself some emotional slack while making the emotionally liberating distinction between fault and blame. Much of psychotherapy is teaching: educating clients how to more fully accept themselves. When they realize that you are

on the side of identifying faults but not blaming individuals for their deficiencies they are more likely to admit to their shortcomings. Thus they have their foot in the door toward either correcting their faults or more peacefully coexisting with them when human limitations block correction. Dousing rather than fanning the flames of client self-blame can be accomplished with some of the following rational inquiry samples:

- "Would my thinking that you are to blame necessarily make it so?"
- "What do you think is more important, what I think or what you think about the matter?"
- "What do you think would be the advantages of owning up to your faults without blaming yourself for having them?"
- "What do you think life would be like if you consistently tendered the idea 'Identify my faults, yes! Blame myself for having them, no!'"
- "How does it follow that if one is at fault one is then blameworthy?"
- "How would you describe to a friend the difference between fault and blame?"
- "Where does blaming yourself for your faults really get you?"
- "What do you think of the notion that if you don't blame yourself for your errors and faults you will then likely make them *less* often?"

43. "But what if I'm embarrassed?"
     Most people can benefit from learning that, although they experience feelings in a social situation, the situation doesn't cause their feelings. "Moments of embarrassment" do not exist; rather, this awkward feeling is created by what a person tells him/herself about the unusual moment. It need not be a foregone conclusion that making a public blunder leads to feelings of embarrassment. Clients can be instructed to understand that, although they experience feelings of embarrassment in a social circumstance, the social arena did not arouse such unwanted emotion. Furthermore, they can be advised that

if they do wrongly make themselves feel embarrassed about their public pitfall, (a) they can tolerate such queasiness rather than despise such discomfort, and (b) they are not bad people for badly embarrassing themselves. Convincing clients to use the moments during which they create embarrassment to work on their own mental health generally, and toleration for and acceptance of themselves specifically, can be done by using some of the following rational alternative questions and statements:

- "What do you think your making yourself feel embarrassed would tell you about you?"
- "How could you still accept yourself even if you foolishly made yourself feel embarrassed?"
- "What do you think would happen to your feelings of embarrassment if you accepted yourself with them?"
- "Is it sacred that you not embarrass yourself?"
- "How could you tolerate embarrassment if you did send it your way?"
- "What is the worst thing that could happen if you did create this embarrassing state?"
- "What do you think is the net effect of your insisting that you absolutely must not feel embarrassment?"
- "What are some things that you could tell yourself to cushion, if not dissolve, feelings of embarrassment?"
- "Were there ever times where you were able to put your foot on the brakes rather than the gas pedal of embarrassment, and if so what did you tell yourself to accomplish this?"

44. "But what if I offend somebody?"
    Because humans tend to exaggerate the impact they have on others, a sense of humility can be an emotional lifesaver in many situations. Clients can be taught more accurately what they can and can't do to another person; that others have free will and can choose whether they are going to personalize your comments and actions. Events close to each other don't necessarily cause each other, and just because you talk or act in contrast to another's values and the other feels hurtfully offended,

does not mean that you caused such a mood in them. To help clients better appreciate that they don't have the all-powerful capability to transplant feelings into another, and do not have to become unduly concerned about the possibility of others putting their guard up in the aftermath of their disapproved-of ways, use the following rational retorts:

- "Why do you think one person will feel offended by another's comment and another will not feel the least bit offended about the same comment?"
- "How can one person offend another without the other's cooperation?"
- "Do you think it's possible to transplant an emotion into someone else?"
- "Do you think others have the free will to choose their response to your disagreeing ways?"
- "If someone would take offense to your tact and/or tactics how could you accept and better tolerate such a disappointing occurrence?"
- "Why must others not take offense to your words and deeds?"
- "What do you think would be a wise way to look at another's guardedness and defensiveness?"

45. "What if he/she rejects my request?"
     This question often implies a fear of rejection, that if someone turns down a request he/she is rejecting the person. The response to this question can be an opportunity to teach the client the more rational human relationship principle that all rejection is self-rejection, that though others can select against us and our askings, no one can reject us but ourselves. The self-rejection can be done via the self-statement, "Because my associate badly refused my request, I'm bad." Questions that would promote a more self-accepting, less personalized adaptation include:

- "Does it follow that, if others reject your request, they are rejecting you?"

- "What do you think the notion 'nobody can reject you but you' means?"
- "If someone refuses your friend's request, are they in fact rejecting your friend?"
- "What is the very worst thing that could happen if your request were rejected?"
- "How have you made yourself feel in the past when others rejected your request?"
- "What are some ways of looking at another's refusal that would allow you to cope more adequately with their contrary response?"

46. "Do I have to do it?"

     Perhaps the core idea underlying better servicing one's emotional well-being is that "nothing in life has to be"; you don't even have to survive—you choose to survive. Such permissive, nondemanding thinking lends itself to increased clearheadedness. Responding to this question with some of the following questions/statements can set the stage for the client's generating self-administered emotional slack. Spelling out to the client that if he does something, e.g., his therapy homework, because he thinks that he absolutely must or has to, he will damn himself whether he does or doesn't do it. If he does the homework out of insistence, he will likely create resentment within himself because he thinks an arbitrary authority says he "has to." On the other hand, if he doesn't do his homework but believes he "has to," "should" or "must" do it, he will likely make himself feel guilty for disobeying an alleged universal standard. The following questions/statements are designed to encourage the client to take the essentialness out of his values to pave the way for diminishing the emotional upheaval in his life:

- "What do you think of the idea that nothing in life has to be—you don't even have to survive, you choose to survive?"
- "What do you think are the advantages of not attaching absolutes to your considerations?"
- "There are no universal laws that I know of."

- "What do you think would be a better way to pose your options to yourself, 'what do I have to do' or 'what would I like to do'?"
- "Describe your feelings when you tell yourself 'I have to do it' compared to your feelings when you say 'I want to do it.'"
- "Do you see where 'I have to' leaves you with no alternatives?"
- "Would it be fair to say that leading with a 'have to' defies free will?"
- "How might thinking you 'have to' do something a certain way stifle creativity and personality well-roundedness?"

47. "Why can't it be easier?"
    Persuading clients that it's not easy to take the easy way out is not an easy task. Motivation by immediate comfort and convenience is the trademark of practically all humans. This question posed by clients implies that (a) a given task must be made easier and (b) there is a specific formula for doing so. Forging ahead with a different focus that discourages a worship of the god called ease is seen in the following rational disputations:

- "How do you lead yourself to believe that there is a special reason (why it can't be easy)?"
- "It could be easier, but that is a far cry from it should or has to be."
- "Because the conditions of life apparently aren't coming together to make it so."
- "Perhaps because many, if not most, things in life that are good for us are hard to do?"
- "Can you think of any advantages that exist as a result of the fact that it isn't easier?"
- "Is it possible that, if the task were made easier, you would appreciate the results less?"
- "It could be easier, but must it be?"
- "Is it necessary for you to know why the task can't be easier before you begin to put your shoulder to the wheel?"
- "Will you wait for it to be easier or are you willing to start on it now?"

- "Would you agree that, once your perspiration creates inspiration, the effort required to accomplish a desirable result will likely seem easier?"

48. "But I wasn't brought up that way."
    There are two types of values, those that your parents acclaimed as befitting for life and those that you developed on your own. Most people don't get themselves too far past the first type. Rather than suggestibly and gullibly accepting values that are handed to them, clients can learn the value of carving out their own. To make oneself a clone of one's upbringing is to stifle other more well-rounded personality potentials. To limit oneself to what one is spoon-fed is to block sampling other choices from life's smorgasbord. Blind acceptance of original parental premises can be discouraged by some of the following rational promptings.

- "If you were brought up to eat manure would you be required to eat it today?"
- "Do you want to live your life by how past arbitrary authority thought you 'should' or how you presently choose to?"
- "What do you think of the idea that, because you live with the consequences of your decisions, it would be advisable to consider making your own choices rather than letting what past arbitrary authorities thought you 'should,' 'must,' or 'ought to' decide?"
- "What do you think life would be like if there were a universal law that said you must follow your upbringing?"
- "What are some disadvantages of giving blind adherence to the past?"
- "Which is a better way to look at life, 'to thine past be true' or 'to oneself be true'?"
- "What would life be like if you put a dent in the sacredness of past values?"
- "Do you wish to live the present as the past or live in a way that remains to be seen what you can bring to your present and future?"

- "Which is better, to live in a manner that is a reenactment of the past or to live in a way that brings options and choices to the present?"
- "Do you believe in the idea that, especially when it is to your advantage to do so, anything you believed in the past, you can disbelieve in the present?"
- "Now that it has been shown to you by your family of origin how not to treat people, how can you start to develop your own ideas on how to do so?"
- "What is more important, your upbringing or whether or not you decide to carry it on?"

49.   "What happens if I just can't take it?"

"I can't stand-it-itis" lies at the base of this inquiry that is in search for assurance that the discomfort likely to be required to accomplish a sought-after result will be within acceptable limits. A protest against the reality that it might not be is figured into this sulky question. Addressing this inquiry in a manner that discloses the underlying problem of low frustration tolerance and its accompanying demand for comfort can be seen in these alternative thoughts and questions:

- "What does the idea 'you can stand anything as long as you're alive' mean for you?"
- (Humorously) "Then you will just have to die from it."
- "What other circumstances in your life have you thought you 'couldn't take' but you still came through above ground?"
- "Is this situation intolerable or just difficult?"
- "How do people manage to push themselves through circumstances that they originally thought they, for the life of them, couldn't take?"
- "It may then become necessary to start over, hopefully with a new beginning."
- "Who knows what would happen? What do you say you cross that bridge *if* and when you come to it?"
- "You can almost always bow out of harm's way as a last resort."

50. "What if it isn't the right solution?"
Often there is no right or wrong solution, THE answer, but simply answers based on present evidence. What is right or wrong varies with time, place, and person yet clients frequently are in desperate search for absolute correctness. Responses to this near-impossible question can assist clients to taper and temper their insistence for surety, certainty, and orderliness in a world where there is none. The following responses can be a lesson in encouragement to develop the tolerance and acceptance that would be helpful in forging ahead with life's ambitions without any assurances of success:

- "Then you would have failed at knowing today's answers, yesterday."
- "You could chalk it up as a learning experience and apply what you learned today, tomorrow."
- "You could figure out how your failed choice could eventually bring you to success."
- "Then you have given yourself practice in being decisively independent in your decision making."
- "You could strengthen your resolve to use better judgment in the future."
- "You could be happy that you had enough guts to decide, yet still acknowledge your disappointment of the results of your choice."
- "Ask yourself 'How have the bad results of my decision been good for me?'"
- "How did your testing the waters help you to deal with the world from a strengthened position in the future, even though you failed to navigate them successfully in the present?"
- "Do you think you can avoid making the wrong decision by not deciding?"
- "You could do at least four things that would have potential benefit for your happiness and survival: accept yourself, tolerate the adversity stemming from your choice, be fair to yourself by not taking a bad situation and making it worse or dupli-

cating it, or count on yourself to cope with the matter in the present and to potentially do better in the future."

51. "Why do I have to suffer?"
    This long-suffering question bemoans the reality that it is par for the human-condition course to be treated unfairly much of the time. Introducing to clients the value of taking the pout out of getting what they don't want or not getting what they do want can be done by an interchange of thinking that examines possible helpful and emotionally healthy responses as opposed to more common moaning-and-groaning rejoinders. Examples of responses that counteract anguishing tendencies are:

- "Can you think of ways to help yourself to be a less active participant in your own suffering?"
- "Do you think there are people who live in a world without suffering?"
- "Which is worse, suffering or making yourself suffer about your suffering?"
- "What leads you to believe that there must be a special reason for your state of deprivation?"
- "What do you think of the idea of 'being worthy of your suffering'—meaning learning something from it?"
- "Are you in the world to not suffer or are you in it to experience it, including doses of suffering?"
- "What are some 'suffering-less' thoughts that would help to lessen rather than increase the pangs of suffering?"
- "What are some good and not-so-good ways to handle suffering?"
- "It may well be one of the hazards of being human."

52. "Why can't I get what I deserve?"
    There is often a discrepancy between what one wants and what one gets. This is bad enough, but when one introduces a philosophy of deservingness in an effort to match up wishes and realities, self-pity will likely enter the picture. The vast majority of humans believe themselves to be special and conclude that, because they are

so special, the universe owes them special favors. Because much emotional disturbance stems from a flawed philosophy of deservingness, leading clients to see the reality that there is no evidence they are owed or entitled to anything can prove fruitful. The sooner they understand *and* accept this fact, the sooner they will be better off emotionally. Squelching emotional disturbance by squelching mandates for deservingness can be done with some of the following methods of thought:

- "Specialness implies anointment; anointment implies deservingness—there is evidence that humans are unique and they would do well to appreciate this fact, but there is no proof for specialness or anointment—so far as we know."
- "Have there been times when you got what you deserved and you wished you wouldn't have?"
- "Because you get what life circumstances produce, not what you want or think that you deserve."
- "Because you apparently haven't been able to convince the universe to give you what you have concluded that you deserve."
- "Perhaps because unfairness is the rule rather than the exception, the norm not the unusual."
- "Because at this point in time what you have insisted that you deserve hasn't evolved or been produced "
- "Because the world doesn't run in orderly cycles and consequently often doesn't present what you have worked long and hard for."

53. "Why me?"
    This dandy is perhaps the most common grandiose off-the-cuff comment in response to expected life circumstances that fizzle. Grandiosity is implied as it is almost as if the person being disadvantaged or selected against is thinking "I must be the one person in the universe who doesn't often come up against adversity" and "Everything I want in life must be and everything that I don't want must not be." This I-am-the-center-of-the-universe

mentality can be forcefully contradicted with the following divergences:

- "Why must adversity avoidance be made unique to you, and only you?"
- "Because the conditions of life came together to produce an accident and you just happened to be in it."
- "Is there any special reason 'why not, not you'?"
- "Because one of the risks of being human is the accessibility to dangers and accidents."
- "Because 'what is' constitutes the entry fee for being an imperfect person, flanked by imperfect people, surrounded by an imperfect world."
- "Consider it a welcome to the club of the human race."
- "Because the next time you experience serenity will be when you're six feet under–the last time, as you may or may not recall, was before you were born!"
- "Because it doesn't say 'hassle-free' on your birth certificate."
- "So that you can make the choice to break down in response to adversity, or break records in spite of it."

54. "That would feel phony and out of character for me."
    One price to pay for personal change is the feeling of discomfort that often accompanies doing something different for the first time. Unless such feelings of strangeness, nervousness, and awkwardness are accepted as being pipers to pay for personal development efforts, the client may beg off attempting to do better by mislabeling his entry-fee discomfort as being phony. When clients are active-directively tutored to (a) not inaccurately label their new efforts as phony but simply as common human feelings that often accompany doing something different and (b) stay with the fear of discomfort until repeated, purposeful exposure to it numbs its terrors, they often can get themselves past their resistance to discomfort barriers. A line of questioning that counters this discomfort-facing reluctance would include the following directives and inquiries:

- "Think of a time in your life that you felt queasy about doing something for the first time. What was it like the second time, fifth time, five-hundredth time?"
- "How could you not stop yourself from taking your nervousness with you to your project, and what do you think that would be like?"
- "Are you being phony or is your uncomfortableness simply the price you're paying for change?"
- "How does one change for the purpose of gaining never-before advantages without acting out of character?"
- "Where has acting *in* character gotten you?"
- "By being willing to act phony en route to changing yourself you are making an honest effort to do so."
- "Little gain without pain, including the pain of self-consciousness related to putting yourself out on a limb—where much of the fruit is."

55. "But I could hurt him/her by doing that."
    Flattery will get you nowhere! No one has ever invented a way to squirm inside someone else's gut and administer a feeling. If we could give each other feelings we could pass along happy feelings to one another for the rest of our lives. Taking on an exaggerated sense of responsibility for others' feelings often blocks assertive action. There is much value in teaching clients that, although they can displease others enormously, it is the receiver of the bad tidings who decides the degree of personalized upset that is going to be made of the displeasing act. The following alternatives can be drawn from to counterbalance the inclination to hold oneself accountable for another's feelings:

- "Tell me, how does one magically gain entrance to another's gut and transplant a feeling?"
- "Who do you think is ultimately responsible for any given individual's feelings?"
- "What do you think of the phrase 'my sticks and stones may break others' bones but my refusing words will never harm

them—unless they sharpen them up and stick them in themselves'?"

- "What would be the advantages of addressing having a sense
  of humility about what you can and can't do to another person?"
- "Do you think another's feelings of hurt are more reflective of
  your inconveniencing them or their thinking about your inconvenient act?"
- "Do you believe others have free will generally and in how
  they interpret your highly dissatisfying acts specifically?"
- "Why would some people feel hurt after being selected against
  by you, and others wouldn't for the same discriminating act?"
- "What advice would you provide a friend who came to you
  claiming he felt hurt due to someone else's attitude and/or behavior toward him?"
- "Hurt mainly constitutes self-blame and self-pity; how could
  your associate not blame or pity himself about your displeasing proclamations?"

56. "How can I get my head on straight?"
    This client-presenting problem would do well to be put
    into a different, unconfusing context. Vagueness in prob-
    lem solving can be set aside in favor of more direct,
    concrete, hands-on objectives that unravel the complex-
    ity of this foggy inquiry. Problem solving is likely to be
    made into a dangling conversation on the once-over-
    lightly, superficial side, unless more bread-and-butter
    goals are established. A more solid foundation for solu-
    tion finding can be established with some of the follow-
    ing directives:

- "Don't you really mean 'What do I want to do with the time of
  my life that I have left?'"
- "Aren't you really asking 'What advantages do I want to gain
  for myself in the one life that I will likely ever have?'"
- "What are some things that you would like to touch, taste,
  feel, and smell in the time you have left in your life?"
- "I don't think anyone has yet invented a 'head-straightener,'
  but perhaps I can help you to better strive toward your goals

and to overcome obstacles that you put in the way of dealing with your problems."

- "Would helping yourself to establish and move toward specific goals be of assistance in your 'getting your head on straight'?"
- "In your own words, how can you tell whether someone has one's head on straight?"
- "Tell me several things that you could do that you're not doing that would constitute having got your head on straight."
- "What are some things that you are currently doing that are in line with your definition of having your head on straight?"

57. "Wouldn't that be awful if . . . (e.g., I tried and failed, felt uncomfortable, was turned down, was criticized, pulled a public blunder, etc.)"
Teaching clients anti-awfulizing methods goes a long way toward better containing emotional upheaval. To label something as awful is to define something as being beyond reality while almost assuring disturbance. When clients learn that disappointments are not disasters, that sadness is not tragedy, they will begin to douse rather than fan the flames of their emotionalism. Helping clients to escape their tendency to exaggerate the significance of things can be done through utilization of some of the following optional directives:

- "What feelings stem from the word 'awful'?"
- "What would be so bad that you haven't already experienced and survived?"
- "Wouldn't it be fair to say that we often learn a great deal from our most God-'awful' experiences?"
- "'Awful' is usually meant to construe an experience as being 100 percent bad—scientifically nothing is 100 percent."
- "Let's say that you're right and I'm wrong and that something can truly be proven to be 'awful.' What good would it do to awfulize about it?"
- "Would it assist your moods to label a bad experience as 'disappointing,' 'frustrating,' 'undelightful,' 'unfortunate,' 'highly inconvenient,' or 'depriving,' rather than as 'awful'?"

- "Would all people judge your negative experience to be awful?"

58. "How can I get him/her to change?"
    Steering clients away from the impossible mission of "I'll change her" toward the reachable alternative of "I'll change my response to her" is a major task of psychotherapy. Until clients accept that the enemy is not so much their partner but more their faulty response to their partner, they will likely continue to play God while fighting like the devil. Promoting a structure of responsibility for individual self can be accomplished by active-directively applying some of the following dictums:

- "Do you think there is a formula for changing another human being?"
- "Have you ever met a person who has changed another person?"
- "Would it be democratic if you could find a way to spoon-feed change to another?"
- "Is there even one shred of evidence that would demonstrate that one person can change another?"
- "What would be your guess as to the long-run effects of forcing someone to change?"
- "What do you think the phrase 'my, how you have changed since I changed' means?"
- "What do you think about using the other's refusal to change as a mechanism to work on your own mental health?"
- "Is it absolutely necessary for the other to change before you can feel better?"
- "Must the other change before you change?"

59. "Wouldn't most people be upset if they were in my shoes?"
    Because humans are remarkably fallible and are prone not only to make mistakes but to not learn from their errors and to therefore *repeatedly* make them, what most people do is nothing to brag about. Showing clients how to be unorthodox so as to better service their emotional well-being is a central goal of helping others. Teaching

them how to resist the normal downstream current of conventional wisdom and to abnormally fight upstream against it is a good example of how persistence against odds can be made to pay off. Because most people would disturb themselves while facing the same adversity is no more to the point than that most people eat fast foods. Each example demonstrates what is normal but is a far cry from illustrating what is healthy. Encouraging clients to go against the wiles of prevailing thought can be suggested via use of some of the following questions and statements:

- "Do you wish to do what most people would do or what you think would be best for you?"
- "Just as people have different size shoes so too are they capable of a different, more helpful and healthful response to the same problem."
- "Do you think Barnum may have underestimated when he said that 'there is a sucker born every minute'?"
- "Would you agree that no one has ever gone broke underestimating the gullibility of the public?"
- "Yes, but is there a universal law that says company has to like and take on others' misery?"
- "Would you prefer to abide by the 'herd mentality' or by 'your mentality'?"
- "Which would be better for you—to be in and of the world or to be just in the world?"
- "Do you want to applesauce your values with the rest or carve out your own distinctive ones?"

60. "Wouldn't you be upset if you were me?"
    To model imperfection by direct and honest responses to this question can discourage client attempts to bestow sainthood on you. Otherwise clients may put themselves down for not being able to measure up to their exalted image of you. Besides, clients are more likely to relate better to someone who is admittedly fallible. Responses

of an up-front, nonsuperficial, modeling-fallibility variety would include:

- "Would it be better for you to try to be more like me, or more like yourself?"
- "Let's say I would upset myself in this situation, as you do and as you have done in similar situations in the past. How would that make it right, better, or the thing to do?"
- "Think and act in your best interest, not as I or anyone else would do."
- "If I would, two wrongs would not by a long shot make a right."
- "If I would blow my brains out would that mean it would be right for you too?"
- "I am, like all humans, as imperfect as the day is long, so better that you set and live your life by your and not my or any other what you view to be Godlike standards."

61. "(Since you know so much about problem-solving) what problems have you overcome in your lifetime?"
Good advice is easier to give than it is to follow. That doesn't mean that it is not good, just difficult to apply. Human service professionals, like all humans, have problems too numerous to mention. When called on to "fess up" to them, rather than indirectly and reflectively hem and haw around this assertive question (e.g., "Why do you ask that question?") put the responsibility for its answer on yourself. Don't dance around; be direct in your response. By doing so you model the transparency you suggest in your clients; demonstrate that you practice the openness that you preach. Albert Schweitzer said, "There's a special kinship between those who bear the mark of pain." Personal sharing allows you to interact with your clients at a deeper level. This breath of fresh air can be injected into the dialogue by use of some of these pronouncements:

- "Almost too numerous to mention, but let me give you a sampling."

- "If you've got the time, I've got the material."
- "What does it mean for you that I've had, am overcoming some, and have not put a dent in other problems of my own?"
- "That is an excellent question and I'm glad that you asked it; I'd be glad to share my emotional well-being batting average with you."
- "One of the reasons that I know so much about problem solving is that I've tried to solve many of my own, for example . . . ."
- "Well, I wasn't exactly born with a glass slipper on my foot or with a silver spoon in my mouth, so therefore I have, on more than one occasion, put my foot in the mouth of my problems—and in some cases have been nearly eaten alive; in other cases I have come out relatively unscarred."

62. "Why doesn't life add up?"
    Incongruities by the armful abound and to better learn how to tolerate and accept those matters that don't seem to make much sense will create a less stressful existence. This question implies an addendum: "Why doesn't life add up—my way?" Redirect this latter insistence with the following modes of disputation:

- "In part due to the random universe in which we live."
- "Because different people are playing different games."
- "Because there is no scorekeeper."
- "What would be required to occur before life would add up for you?"
- "Because there is no formula that fits for the wishes of all."
- "When someone says 'life doesn't add up' what they often mean is 'I'm not getting my own way—as I must. Is this the case with you?"
- "Need there be a special reason for such an imbalance?"
- "If there were a special reason, would that change the facts or your mechanisms of coping with them?"

63. "Why won't others cooperate?"
    Clients practically always insist that the world and people in it have to cooperate before they can better their plight. Consequently, they live their lives on a shoestring and

make themselves beholden to others' support prior to forging ahead on their own behalf. Pointing out to clients the advisability of emotional self-reliance so as not to put oneself at the mercy of others can be accomplished by forthrightly leading with the following conclusions:

- "Apparently their batteries operate on free will and not your will."
- "Due to the fact of one person's cup of tea often being another's poison."
- "Because humans tend to go in the direction they're headed, not in the one you're headed."
- "Great minds don't always think alike."
- "Different people, different agendas."
- "Because they are too busy following their noses and not yours."
- "Because they often assume that the world was made for them and not for you."
- "Maybe it's because you don't run them or the universe–yet."
- "If and when you see things their way they will likely start to cooperate."
- "Because you have not yet tickled their ears enough."

64. "I can't say no."

Disapproval anxiety and low frustration tolerance are contained in this rationalization for inaction, e.g., "If I refused another's request she might not like me and I couldn't stand that or the discomfort that would accompany such refusal." Guilt as a special form of anxiety comes from the belief that saying no is an unauthorized act and therefore you "should" not do so. Getting clients to authorize themselves to refuse requests when it is in their best interest to do so can assist in overcoming the more general problem of self-blame. Enlightened self-interest, whereby the client puts himself first and others a close second, rather than others first and himself a distant second, is a major therapeutic goal that can be sought by persuading the client to say no, preferably without feeling guilty, but also taking the guilt with him if necessary. In the latter case, an immunity to feeling guilt is likely to be developed after repeated exposure to putting one's better foot forward. The following directives try to open up alternatives by taking the "can't" out of the original declaration and replacing it with a more permissive view:

- "You can't say no because if you did . . . ."
- "What is the worst thing that has befallen you after saying no?"
- "Go over to the corner of this room and stand on your head." (Client inevitably says 'no,' thus disproving the hypothesis that he 'can't' say no.)
- "Think of someone you know who seems to give himself very little problem about saying no. What would you guess are some of the secrets to his success?"
- "Let's say ten people receive the same request and all are reluctant to say no, but five say no and five say yes. Explain the different responses to the same request."
- "If I gave you one hundred dollars would you say no?"
- "Is it more that you 'can't' say no or is it that you 'won't'?"
- "Do you think of the advantages of selectively refusing others requests? What are some?"

65. "What should I do about this?"
    Clients like to be taken by the hand while making choices. They often look to their counselor as an authority on what will be a surefire decision regarding matters of concern. Routing clients toward making their own choices rather than depending on you to make them is a pivotal part of encouraging self-responsibility. Helplessness is discouraged and self-responsibility is encouraged by zeroing in on the following rational explanations and promptings:

- "Do you believe there is a recipe for making this decision?"
- "Keep in mind that being able to do this or that is light-years apart from the idea that therefore you should."

- "What is more important—what I think the right decision might be, or what you have a sneaking suspicion that it is?"
- "Do you think that I know what would be best for tomorrow, today?"
- "What conclusions have you drawn so far from the pros and cons that you have itemized?"
- "If I told you my thoughts on the matter, would you actually follow them?"
- "Tell me more about what you mean by 'should.'"
- "Is there ever a precise, exact way to do anything you have a yen for?"

66. "People never understand me."
    Accepting what a rare commodity understanding is, is no easy task. Teaching clients how to live reasonably happily without steady doses of this comforting experience is one of the frequently overlooked goals of psychotherapy. Believing oneself to be understood by another is a pleasurable experience; not overreacting when not understood is that much better. That way clients can avoid making themselves out to be the playthings of others' understanding—or lack thereof. Getting at and over clients' dire need for understanding can be done with the following countering ideas:

- "People never understand you so therefore . . . ."
- "'Never' is an everlasting term. Do you think that you might be pouring it on a little thick as to what you are more precisely up against?"
- "What do you think is more important, others' lack of understanding or the conclusions you draw about their misunderstandings?"
- "Let's assume you're correct, that *nobody ever* understands you. What are some ways that you could devise to cope with that reality?"
- "Understanding is nice—but is it necessary?"
- "Do you *need* to be understood by others?"

- "Are there ways that you contribute to making it difficult for others to understand you?"

67. "How do you think I feel when every time I try, I fail?" Disputing at practically every turn clients' sloppy thinking that attributes their feelings to external causes is a primary, ongoing therapeutic task. If it were the failure per se that caused the implied unwanted feelings, these could be contained only by producing indefinite successes—hardly a human possibility! Getting away from the guesswork requested and into the role of teaching the anatomy of emotions, what causes them, and how they can be controlled, is the task of the helper. The positioning of this question also affords the helper the opportunity to get at the exaggerated, absolutistic inference, e.g., the "every time" component of it. In that emotional disturbance is largely caused by cognitive distortion, seeking semantic precision in an effort to better regulate emotional upset is a higher-order task of teaching and reaching more frequent emotional self-control. The following comments and questions can contribute to that end:

- "Don't you mean how do I think you make yourself feel when you try and fail?"
- "Different people respond differently to the same failure. Why do you think that is so?"
- "How do you make yourself feel when you fail and would you be interested in learning how to make yourself feel any different?"
- "In my view, how you would make yourself feel even after repeated failures would mainly depend on what you would tell yourself about your coming up short."
- "Do you think that 'every time' is a slight exaggeration on your part that might contribute to continued failings and unwanted feelings?"
- "It may depend on how much you are able to get yourself to focus on the advantages of failure and even perhaps the disadvantages of success."

- "It sounds like whatever that feeling might be you don't like it and may be interested in learning how to change it, is that so?"

68. "It didn't work, I told you it wouldn't."
    This I-told-you-so message may be a confrontive attempt by clients to challenge, if not to get you on the defensive, in being accountable for the negative outcome of their efforts. Sprightly nondefensive responses that prevent the transfer of responsibility for the clients' decision to try suggested homework assignments gone awry would be in order. Responses that would demonstrate this "best defense as being a good offense" principle include:

- "OK, you're telling me so. Now what did you say to yourself about the homework assignment that may have contributed to its downfall?"
- "Keep in mind 'it,' meaning your homework, won't so much work for you as much as you work for it."
- "Ask not what your homework can do for you, ask what you can do for your homework."
- "What did you learn from this backfiring that you may not have learned had you succeeded?"
- "Would it have been better to not try and fail as you didn't, or to try and fail as you did?"
- "Is it possible that part of the problematic outcome stems from your 'self-fulfilling promise' philosophy. As you indicate in your question you nearly promised yourself it wouldn't work before you even tried."
- "Now that you first didn't succeed, are you willing to try and try again?"
- "Let's assume you were right and I was wrong, what would life be like if next time it were the other way around?"

69. "Why can't I get better any faster?"
    Tapering clients' unrealistic expectations is a frequent therapeutic endeavor. Achieving a balance between assuming that because the problem took a long time coming it will absolutely take a month of Sundays to correct it, and insisting on a quick, easy fix whereby happiness is

achieved in a twinkling of an eye, allows for realistic problem solving minus the rose garden to go with it. When educated, clients will often accept that their unwanted choice-blocking emotions, e.g., anger, depression, guilt, fear, and anxiety, are not like a light switch that can be turned off and on, but more like a light dimmer that can dim and better control feelings, but not instantly evaporate them. Getting clients past "patience, crap—I'm going to kill someone" to patience as a virtue, including the patience that allows changed feelings and behaviors to catch up to changed thoughts and new philosophies, can be a helping endeavor. Buying time and patience can be accomplished by including some of the following comments and questions:

- "Because human emotion can't be turned off like hot and cold running water."
- "Perhaps because your expectations were too unrealistic to begin with."
- "Haste can sometimes make waste and if you had more of a conversion experience—a quick fix—you might find that the changes made would be less likely to stand the test of time."
- "If I had a light dimmer in my office I could dim the lights and that apparently is the best you can do for now, dim rather than dissolve your feelings."
- "How fast would be fast enough as far as lessening the frequency, strength, and length of your upset?"
- "Because you're a limited human being, deficient at going any faster for now."
- "Due to your and nature's inability to produce the conditions that would allow for a speedier emotional recovery."
- "Slow but sure is better, just like the turtle that beat the hare to the finish line."
- "It could be because you're doing some of the wrong things in your efforts to feel better."
- "Because this is the closest you are able to get yourself to the bull's-eye for now."

70. "The world and people in it seem to be against me."
Teaching clients to understand and accept life in a random, impartial universe is a major asset for minimizing anxiety and anger. Addressing the fact that the universe is objective—that others are for themselves rather than against us and that it would therefore behoove us to adopt a philosophy of enlightened self-interest—is reflected in the following rebuttals:

- "What is more important, the world and others seemingly being against you or you being for yourself?"
- "Would that not be all the more reason for you to be for yourself?"
- "What leads you to believe that others are more against you than for themselves?"
- "How would you cause yourself to feel if you understood and accepted life and the people in it to be more for themselves than against you?"
- "Are there any exceptions to your stated position?"
- "How do you conclude that others have nothing else better to do than to try to do you in?"
- "What are you doing at the precise time that the world seems *less* against you that is different from when it seems to be more totally against you?"
- "Do you ever make it a point to pay attention to exceptions to your 'me against the world' conclusion?"

71. "I guess it was never meant to be."
Challenging superstitious thinking practically every time it rears its mystical, ugly head is a task worth attending to, lest clients continue to run their lives on presumptions. Statements such as "It wasn't in the cards," "If it were meant to be—it would have been," and "It wasn't earmarked for success" sound good and provide a degree of immediate comfort in the aftermath of failing, but in the long run strengthen a fatalistic, deterministic outlook about life. After all, why bother to try if there is a master of your fate whose whims you are subject to? Such fictitious ramblings are often made into excuses for not roll-

ing up your sleeves and getting your teeth into the conditions that would be required to complete to produce a given result. If something is preordained as "meant or not meant to be"—why bother! The following arguments are designed to encourage a more flexible, antideterministic, inconclusive, humanistic outlook en route to cognitive, emotive, and behavioral change:

- "Is it that outcomes are not meant to be, or more that you were not able to make them a reality?"
- "Is there any evidence for determinism, that outcomes are determined to be before they are even attempted?"
- "Where does this fate-has-you-by-the-hair position really get you?"
- "Which is likely to create more incentive, 'it might not be meant to be', or 'it will likely be what I make it to be'?"
- "Do you favor free will or determinism?"
- "Is it more helpful to believe 'that's the way the cookie crumbles' or 'that's the way I make it crumble'?"
- "What is a better dictate to follow, 'it wasn't in the cards' or 'I did not play my cards right (but can perhaps do better with my next hand)'?"

72. "Why does that always get me upset?"
    This question contains perhaps the two major faulty inferences of humans: that scientifically something can be 100 percent, and that outside forces are the cause of emotions running rampant. If emotions are philosophically based it would be important to debate clients' dogmatic ideas that something absolutely occurs each and every time a given situation presents itself and that the occurrence "gets" the client upset and is therefore responsible for emotional outcome. These common themes are contained in many of the difficult questions and statements frequently posed by clients and can be clarified and disputed with these and other similar countering messages:

- "Would it be more accurate to ask "How come I *often get my-self* upset about that?"
- "Who do you think is ultimately responsible for an individual's emotions?"
- "Is there any part of your question that might be more than a slight exaggeration?"
- "If things truly do upset you, how could you ever have a snowball's chance in Haiti of changing unless matters of the world and people in it change first?"
- "Can you provide evidence to support your contentions that 'always' is a provable description and that forces outside of you 'get' you upset?"
- "What are the emotional leftovers from such fatalistic, finalis-tic, outer-directed philosophies?"
- "Do you believe that there are exceptions to practically every rule and that the individual can have a say-so in activating those exceptions?"
- "Do you think that the way a person describes the origin of a problem and its frequency is a factor in his/her feelings about it?"
- "How can you keep your perceptions of the extent and cause of your emotions within more hopeful and helpful bound-aries?"

73. "I won't ever be happy until I get over this."
     Establishing preconditions for happiness can make its attainment difficult, especially if those conditional judg-ments are outside the lines of reality. To "get over" something is an all-or-nothing term that doesn't consider (a) that you likely wouldn't want to "get over" losses and adversities because leftover feelings of sadness about these experiences allow you to more keenly appreciate your values, (b) if you were able to completely "get over" a negative happening you would learn little if any-thing from the experience, and (c) to put your emotional well-being on hold until hell freezes over or until you "get over" a dissatisfying happening, whichever comes first, is a poor substitute for forging ahead with—or with-out—getting over the adversity of concern. You don't have

to wait for what you would consider a successful resolution of the problem before you can go ahead without it! This is an especially valuable message to give to clients in that often, in spite of the best therapeutic intentions, the long and short of the helping-process outcome is that due to her fallible nature the client will be required to learn how to better coexist with the undesirable emotional and/or behavioral problem rather than "get over" it in a herculean fashion. Retorts designed to make the client more aware of his self-imposed restrictions to a happier existence include:

- "Would you be willing to start by simply making yourself less miserable?"
- "It sounds like you're giving yourself a signed, sealed, and delivered guarantee."
- "Is it necessary to whitewash your past adversity before you can help yourself to at least some semblance of happiness?"
- "Can you not feel better in certain ways even though you are still making yourself feel unhappy in a different way?"
- "Are there not other ways of creating happiness aside from getting yourself past this particular problem?"
- "Because one part of your life is yet unfulfilled are you required to make yourself nearly completely unhappy?"
- "What is the point in your sealing off other possibilities for happiness simply because you are unable to move a certain mountain?"
- "What good does it do to put your life on hold until a certain thorn in your side can be removed?"
- "Are there other unhappy events of your life that you have not gotten yourself over but yet you have been able to pull off at least a modicum of happiness in spite of that disappointment?"

74. "Can't you just tell me what to do?"
    Clients' self-discovery in solving their own problems is desirable, though not always reachable. This does not mean that client self-creation of solutions should not be sought after as the preferable vehicle of progress. Dependency

on a higher authority as one's guiding light is a temptation often too immediately convenient for clients to resist. The answer to this question—"yes and no"—"yes, I could simply tell you what to do, but no, I won't because that won't help you to become more of an independent problem-solver," would do well to be conveyed to clients with some of the following declaratives:

- "Is your goal to make yourself more, or less, dependent on external authority?"
- "Which do you think is better for you, to stand on your own two feet in making choices or to lean on me to make them for you?"
- "Let's brainstorm alternatives that you can draw from."
- "If you unthinkingly turn the decision over to me, how will that make you a better thinker?"
- "Blind allegiance to my directions won't help you to see the value of thinking for yourself."
- "I could, but how would that be helpful to you as a future problem solver?"
- "Your request implies that I would then be responsible for the outcome of my advice—assuming that you would actually take it."
- "How might that make it simple and convenient for you in the short run but be against your best interests in the long run?"

75. "Isn't there an easier way?"
    Distinguishing with clients the difference between the long easier and the short harder way is perhaps the most important agenda item in meeting and beating client resistance to change. Taking a long-range view of life can be prompted by instructing clients to stop and ask themselves "Where will this get me?" and "Do I want to feel better right now by taking the short harder way, or do I want to feel better for the rest of my life by following the long easier way?" A seeming paradoxical answer to this question often determines whether the fork-in-the-road decision is going to follow the lines of doing what is in one's eventual better interests. The main cause of client resistance is (de)motiva-

tion by low frustration tolerance (LFT) or dramatically expressing the difficulty one will experience while completing a given project. Such theatrics along with the demand for ease can be discouraged by some of the following disputations:

- "What do you think of the idea that 'a shortcut is the longest distance between two points'?"
- "It's often not easy to take the easy way out."
- "What would it mean for you if there weren't an easier way?"
- "In your experience, how often are there easier ways to do things that are of great benefit to you?"
- "Often insisting upon an easier way results in running in circles due to cutting corners."
- "How important do you make it for yourself to find an easier way before you give it the old college try?"
- "Easier methods often are akin to lackadaisical ones, which will likely get one no place fast!"
- "Gaining, maintaining, and sustaining constructive action are usually on the other side of 'easier does it.'"

76. "But he/she has no right!"
    Accepting others' rights to trespass on clients' values is practically always a bitter pill for them to swallow, but when taken increases tolerance and acceptance levels on the way down. Until others' violation of seemingly sacred values can be better stomached, emotional indigestion in the form of anger, resentment, and vindictiveness will likely continue to dominate. Forcefully promoting the idea that due to free will and human limitations others have a right to (a) be wrong, (b) purposefully, willfully, intentionally be wrong, and (c) not learn from their mistakes and therefore repeatedly make them, can go a long way toward reducing friction between clients and their social group. From there, bigger, better, and more civilized ways of relating can be put into gear. The following divergencies can help supplant the

notion that others have no right to go against what one believes to be the absolute truth:

- "Where is it written that others have no right to thwart and balk at your values and to intentionally do so?"
- "Whose law of the land are you operating under?"
- "Can your declaration be fully documented?"
- "Says who?"
- "Must he/she only do things that you have granted entitlement for?"
- "If you were general manager of the universe what rights would you bestow on this individual?"
- "Who establishes 'rights' around here anyway?"
- "Would there ever be any circumstances in which you would consider this person to have a right to do what he is doing or to not do what he isn't doing?"
- "Would it be better to believe that you wish he would love and honor your opinions as to what is best rather than that he has no right not to?"

77. "Why do I have to be so different?"
     Humans tend to assume the accuracy of their misery equation: "My differences from others = my worthlessness." Do not allow clients to define themselves by their differences from the majority in their social group without a good persuasive fight. The therapist cannot stand idly by while emotional disturbance is made to escalate. Helping clients come to terms in an emotionally healthy way with their peculiarities and oddities minimizes shame and self-depreciation, both of which will multiply original problems and upsets. The following persuasions can help in containing such problems:

- "Because this is apparently the nature of the beast."
- "How has it been to your advantage to be so set apart from others?"
- "Because you're unique. Now how can you better appreciate your uniqueness without defining yourself by it?"

- "Who are some people who would be considered to be highly unusual by most, but whom you respect a great deal?"
- "What recommendations would you give to others who shared your distinctiveness?"
- "What leads you to believe that there is a special reason?"
- "Because you are what yourself and others might call abnormal does this mean that you have to deal with it in unhealthy ways?"
- "Aren't you really assuming that being normal or like most others is something to brag about?"
- "How does it follow that because most people are not the way you are that they are holier than thou and you are unworthier than all?"

78. "How can I get them to like me?"
    Disapproval trepidations lie at the core of much anxiety. Curtailing clients' overconcern about what others think about them frees them emotionally so that they can then enjoy slices of life that they ordinarily have avoided. Persuade clients to give up their need for approval so they can be themselves, rather than prove themselves, within their social group. This will provide greater informality, give and take, rotation, and balance with others. The following rational statements and explanations will help clients be true to themselves and avoid patronizing others to gain approval:

- "Consider the possibility that you may not be able to do so, what would that mean for you?"
- "Are there limitations to how far you would go to accomplish that?"
- "Let's say that there was an instance where you were not willing to meet the requirements of another's approval. What could you tell yourself so as to not unduly upset yourself about deficiencies in gaining it?"
- "Which is better, to be true to yourself and chance others' disapproval or to provide false flattery in hopes of gaining another's liking?"

- "Find out what pleases them enormously, make a strenuous effort to establish those provisions–but consider the price of such labor if it is incompatible with your values."
- "Do you want them to approve or do you think you absolutely require their approval?"
- "How important is it for you to achieve this goal?"
- "If doing handstands and/or cartwheels were in order, would you do them?"
- "Do you mean *get* them to like you, or do you mean invite, encourage, make it convenient for them to like you?"
- "What are some things that you have noticed others were willing to do to gain another's approval that you thought were too high a price and therefore would not be willing to do?"
- "How do you think the idea of 'to thine own self be true' fits into your desired goal?"

79. "When will I ever get better?"
    This common question implies that the client will get better and that there is an identifiable timetable for doing so. It would be well for clients to be introduced to the reality that (a) rather than getting better at reducing their symptoms the best they can often do is to learn to better coexist with them and (b) the timetable for such ongoing coping realities may well be, due to the marked fallibility of the human condition, for the rest of one's life. Acceptance is a major change and often the ultimate solution and control factor to many problems of human existence. Getting this across to clients can often do much good by way of taking pressure off themselves for having inevitable problems. The following modes of thought respond to this inquiry in a way that encourages a tolerance buildup for what, despite one's best efforts, may not be able to be changed:

- "Your chances of containing your problems may well be much better than getting over them."
- "Mental health is a lot like dental health–everyone has got a few cavities, rather than it being the absence of not only problems, but *this* problem."

- "You will likely do better with this problem when you complete the conditions necessary to keep it more under wraps."
- "Who is to say that you will ever or never get better?"
- "If your time did not come, how could you do well to accept that?"
- "Would you be willing as an FHB (fallible human being) to settle for 'less worse'?"
- "What would worse coming to worst mean for you and what would the advantages of accepting such a possibility do for you emotionally?"
- "Do you believe it absolutely necessary that you get better and to know when that will be?"

80. "How can I make my child mind me?"

As a group, parents tend to overestimate their impact upon their children. They often assume that if they say and do the wrong thing their child will turn out oppositional. Wrong on both accounts! The best or worst a parent can do is to convenience the child to behave well or to act oppositional. However, chances are better that the child will tend to go in the direction that he/she is headed. By explaining to the child what the consequences are for both good and bad behavior parents can back their good intentions with the right methods, and in doing so complete perhaps the most important parental task—force the child to make a decision as to how he/she wants to live. By informing the child what good consequences can be expected with cooperation and what negative consequences to expect if he/she doesn't play ball—and then backing off and letting the child decide the next move—the parent guarantees the offspring opportunity but doesn't assure success; only the child can do this by making a decision that would be in his/her best interests. My point is that by forcing the child to decide, the parent has fulfilled his/her responsibility in the decision-making act. Rational counters by the counselor that can help provide a realistic perspective to the parenting role include:

- "Perhaps the most you can do is to make it convenient for your child to motivate himself in a way that would be in his best interests; you can do this by telling your child what favorable consequences he can expect if he abides by the house rules, and what unfavorable happenings he can expect if he doesn't comply."
- "You can force your child into making a decision, but you can't force him into making the right one."
- "Mission impossible is to transplant an attitude into your child's head that would be better for him to take on; mission possible is to change your response toward whatever attitude your child decides to give himself."
- "By learning how to get yourself less upset when he doesn't mind you."
- "By understanding and accepting that compliance on his part would be nice but not necessary for your life to go on, you can provide him with less to rebel against."
- "Minding less when he doesn't mind may encourage him to be of a mind to mind you more often."
- "Do you view it as your duty to gain your child's cooperation?"
- "How sacred is it for you, for your child to defer to your rules?"

81. "How can I get him/her to love me?"
Humans naturally attach themselves to another but then often tend to get a little pushy in their efforts to control the other to bond back with them. Rather than be patient in hoping for a return attachment the individual usually tries to do something for another that only the other can do–decide to return the connection. The more the controller tries to "get" the other to reciprocate an attachment the more a case is built for desperation, ultimately contributing to driving the other away. It would be best for the client to be educated that a person can't force another to love him/her; one can only put one's best foot forward in hopes of not getting it stepped on. Alternative responses that encourage clients to maintain their desire

for a return attachment while laying to rest an insistence upon it include:

- "Pleasing enormously another person invites and encourages them to love you, but that is about as far as you can go."
- "If you could 'get' or 'force' another to love you, what do you think would be the long-range result of such coercion?"
- "You can possibly get others to pretend that they love you by putting a gun to their head or threatening them in some other way, but this will likely result in only temporary adulation."
- "You can convenience another's attraction to you by not demanding that attraction."
- "You can invite others to lean toward you by showing an interest in not only what they can do for you, but also by what they can do for themselves."
- "It's hard to resist someone who is more interested in accommodating the relationship than in being right."

82. "What will happen if I lose control over my feelings?"
    The possibility of losing control over runaway emotions is a common client concern. This fear-of-fear phenomenon often goes unexplored, leaving much residual anxiety that serves to maintain the original overreaction. When a client catastrophizes about the initial symptom, symptom despisement gives way to an escalation of the beginning emotional problem. Humans not only upset themselves but upset themselves about upsetting themselves! At the root of such throwing of gasoline at the presenting symptom is a fear of "losing my mind." Until clients can be reassured or convinced that they are not going to end up in a padded cell, or if they literally do end up in a padded cell that such a worst occurrence would be tolerable, they will find much difficulty overcoming their problems and disturbances. Suggested statements, questions, and recommendations that can help to curtail this fear include:

- "Think of the worst emotional overflow you have ever had in your life. How did you cope with that?"

- "One way to gain better control over emotions is to accept it when you don't have better control."
- "How do you think you would feel in such a circumstance if you told yourself, 'I don't have to control my emotions as I would like to'?"
- "In your wildest imagination what would you envision as the worst thing that could occur?"
- "You would feel uncomfortable, perhaps like you never have felt before."
- "Then you would have failed at accomplishing one of your goals, that of not losing control."
- "You would not lose your mind, you would simply experience diminishment of your capacities to regulate your feelings and moods."
- "One thing to avoid is transforming the solution into the problem by insisting that you absolutely must better regulate your discomfort."

83. "I can't just let him fail again."
    Trying to stop others from doing things to themselves that only they can prevent is a common human enterprise. Taking responsibility for others' failures by transplanting the alleged key to success into their lock is one of those efforts in futility that in the end breeds resentment. Encouraging clients to care less, without becoming uncaring, to be realistic and humble in determining what they can and can't do for someone else, can be done by examining some of the following messages:

- "Is your choice to not let him fail or is it whether you're going to hassle him or yourself when he does?"
- "What would life be like if you let yourself not get caught up in trying to succeed for someone else?"
- "How does one intercede and succeed at the same time on another's behalf?"
- "Is it possible to do someone else's work for them?"
- "Good intentions to prompt someone else's success often pave the way to hell."

- "If you could cushion the blow of another's defeat, what would be the disadvantages of such an endeavor?"
- "How can your associate gain a feeling of accomplishment without accomplishing anything due to your intervention?"
- "What would be some drawbacks to depriving another of the right to fail–assuming you could do that?"
- "What do you think would be the resulting fallout for you from your strenuous efforts to protect your associate from himself?"
- "Do you have eventual control over letting another's failure transpire or do you mainly have control over your response to it?"

84. "How do I know if I'm saying the right thing?"
    The perfect words at the perfect time lie somewhere beyond the pot of gold at the end of the rainbow. No matter how carefully you choose your words with another, they are still subject to interpretation. One person's sweet translation is another person's poison. Not knowing the exact right thing to say that would assure a favorable impression usually results in inaction. Such nonexpressiveness is often followed by self-downing for not being among the more assertive postures. Hesitation can be broken by teaching clients to drop their perfectionistic stance that when addressing their views they absolutely must do so at the perfect time, in the perfect manner, accompanied by the perfect message. When clients learn that they would do better to not rate themselves as unworthier than all for their nonexpressions or nonperfectionistic expressions or holier than thou for successfully spouting their message, they will likely be better able to unleash what they have to say. Rational inquiries that would more allow clients to, when in their best interests to do so, unveil their thoughts include:

- "What might be more significant than 'saying the right thing' is what you are telling yourself about the possibility of *not* saying the right thing."
- "Must you know beforehand that you are saying the right thing?"

- "If you did put your foot in your mouth what are some ways you could (a) not put yourself down for doing so and (b) dislodge it from your throat?"
- "In an uncertain world your chances of knowing ahead of time are slim indeed."
- "You can assure yourself of a better opportunity of saying more of the 'right' things by rehearsing ahead of time but it is highly doubtful that opportunity will be perfectly transformed into success."
- "Others will respond unpredictably to the same words."
- "What will it mean for you when you don't say the exact right thing?"
- "Troubling yourself less about saying the wrong things will likely increase your chances of saying more of the right things."

85. "What do I do when I don't know what to do next?"
     Responding to unstructured circumstances is a large part of daily living. Because the world and people in it are ever changing, ambiguous life situations are often thrown our way. Such curve balls become a test of our creativity. Dispelling notions that (a) the client absolutely has to respond, (b) he/she has to do so quickly, and (c) the response of choice must ultimately be the right one, can assist clients to more clearly forge ahead in their decision to respond or not to respond, and with which response. Demonstrating to the client that to put the matter on hold while she continues to try to create the range of responses that might be in her best interests, and not upsetting herself about not knowing what to do right now, can be accomplished with the following observations and dictates:

- "Nonfrantically continue to search."
- "Don't assume that you are required to do anything."
- "Make it a point to not rate yourself by the outcome of what you eventually decide to do or not to do."
- "Consider waiting for something else to unfold before you make your choices."

- "Itemize what you have decided *not* to do and see if you can't transfer ideas from that side of the coin to the other."
- "What are some possible choices of action that you would recommend to an associate in a similar, seemingly dead-end dilemma?"
- "What not to do often is as important as what to do, such as not overreacting to the facts of your uncertainty—otherwise you will give yourself an emotional problem about a practical problem."
- "Try to hold your horses about deciding until more evidence is dished out."
- "Be certain that it's not that you don't know what to do next but that you're not applying what you know because you have convinced yourself that it's too hard or too uncomfortable to put this knowledge into practice."

86. "But I'm not consistent enough at doing better."
    Clients often give up when they don't immediately maximize their goals. Realistic, straightforward information about what to expect from their learning curve can prevent a tapering of interest in persisting with their objectives. Establishing more consistency without insisting upon perfectionism can be reviewed with the client. This can prevent the discouragement that comes from believing that because you are not as consistent as you would like to be at this point in time, that you may as well throw in the towel, bypassing future possibilities of generating more locomotion. The following persuasions can encourage the stamina required to generate eventual greater consistency:

- "The flip side of your inconsistency is that you are trying on your own behalf. What do you think would be the advantages of focusing more on that?"
- "The facts of your inconsistency mean that you are doing something right, some of the time—try to build from those successes."
- "What are some of the things that you have learned from those times you have failed to be consistently successful?"
- "Have you been more consistent than when you first started?"

- "When you have been on target with success what are some of the things that you did right that you would like to more consistently do?"
- "It's good you want to stay on the straight and narrow because if you didn't want to you would have even more problems—just don't expect it to be perfectly straight and exactly narrow."
- "How much, in your view, would be consistent enough?"
- "What are some things that you would like to more consistently do?"

87. "Why can't they give me the benefit of the doubt?"
    In an experiment a large number of people were apologized to by a stranger. There was no previous connection between each person and the unknown individual. Yet, each person accepted the apology as if it was deserved! Likewise, just as the person apologized to responding as if they deserved it, so too do many clients not so secretly harbor the notion that they deserve to be selected toward for no special reason. The above client's question implies a dictate that others most certainly must not waver in favoritism pointed in their direction. There is no special reason that says others can't provide the benefit of the doubt, though there may be many reasons why they won't do so. Helping clients accept that others will often discriminate against them for their own reasons, without explaining their logic beforehand, can be accomplished with the following questions and explanations:

- "Obviously they can or could give you the benefit of the doubt, but is it a necessity that they do?"
- "Because by and large humans will consider first how their decision will be to their own rather than to your advantage."
- "Perhaps because in doing so they would go against themselves."
- "Maybe it's because they believe themselves to have more important things to consider than your conveniences."
- "In part because it's the human condition to be treated unfairly much of the time."

- "How do you make it a problem for yourself when others don't designate you as the primary benefactor of the doubt?"
- "There may well be no special reason for their selecting counter to your benefit."
- "A better question than 'why' can't they give you the benefit of the doubt might be 'what.' What are you going to do to cope better with such a disappointing turn of events."
- "It might be that others couldn't care less about what would be of benefit to you—how does that possibility grab you?"

88. "Why do I have to put up with such nonsense?"
    To be singled out as the one person in the universe who is to be insulated against everyday hassle is the (day)dream of most humans. This demand for immunity from ever-present annoyances amplifies preexisting frustrations in that protests against such irritating realities don't cause them to go away. In fact, such refusals to accept what exists by way of burrs in the saddle invite additional displeasure when others counter these protests with distastes of their own about one's obnoxious insistences. Acceptance of unpleasantries so as not to create a multiplying effect can be done by introducing the following suggested alternatives for viewing frequent nonsensical experiences:

- "What are your other options?"
- "Because you have virtually no control over its existence."
- "Conditions of life sometimes come together to create obnoxious circumstances, leaving you with choices as to how you will cope with them."
- "In some ways because you're an imperfect person, in an imperfect world, flanked if not surrounded by imperfect people—can you beat that?"
- "Because the universe is not providing you with special favors by way of circumventing such befuddlement."
- "As part of the entry fee for remaining above ground."
- "Because you have had your allotment of peace and tranquility—before you were born."

- "So that you can become well practiced, more of the same lies ahead."

89. "How can I be happy?"

    This absolutistic question implies that happiness is a fixed state that you obtain rather than a process that you imperfectly try to maintain. Alternative views of happiness that reflect individual differences, optional feelings, and behavioral states, e.g., meaning and vital absorption, as an ongoing search, directly related to expectations, and varying degrees of this state of mind should be proposed. Plan with clients for opportunities to sink their teeth into a special interest that may help sustain a favorable state of mind. Happiness as paradox–expecting less and getting more–can be sampled. Identifying happiness not as a permanent place you get to and complacently settle in, but as something continually sought after, can be worth exploring. Seeking "happiness" as being perfectionistic and too idealistic while striving to be happ*ier* as being nonperfectionistic and more realistic can be distinguished. The above views can be incorporated in some of the following questions and comments designed to better understand and to more rationally seek this most often temporary, elusive state of consciousness:

- "Bertrand Russell wrote a book called *Conquest of Happiness*. What does that unusual title mean for you?"
- "You could program all your life's events to bend in your favor or you can bend your thinking so as to get yourself less upset when circumstances don't get your seal of approval–which do you think is more accessible?"
- "One person's meat is another person's poison. What is your meat?"
- "One of the secrets to feeling happ*ier* is to not put so much pressure on oneself to be so."
- "If you were chronically happy would you still appreciate the benefits of happiness?"
- "Find something you like doing and identify how it makes a difference in the overall scheme of things."

- "Find a love relationship you're willing to work on and find work that you love."
- "Allow it to be a by-product of your efforts to do what you want and want what you do."
- "To not insist on happiness, to believe that you don't have to be happy, is to convenience its appearances."
- "The less you believe happiness to be essential, essentially the happier you will be."

90. "Because I ask for so little, I should get what little I ask for."
     Watering down your request guarantees virtually nothing by way of a return on your asking. Defining as fair that you get so little because that is all that you asked for and then demanding that this self-created equation become a reality results in wallowing in hurt and self-pity. Steering the clients away from this mythical recipe in order to better service their emotional well-being can be accomplished by use of these confrontive disclaimers and explainers:

- "Is there evidence to support your 'ask a little, get a little' theory?"
- "Who determines and directs that your minute request be granted?"
- "Does this expectation hold true for all that hold to it?"
- "Where does that 'should' get you emotionally?"
- "How does asking make it so?"
- "If you think you are mandated to gain the little bit you asked for, how will you honestly feel those times that you don't bat a thousand in receiving your miniature request?"
- "Aren't you really demanding that a preexisting law of the universe be established just for little bitty old you?"
- "Don't you really mean that the less you ask for the more likely you may gain what you hope for, but that this expectation should not be blown up into a demand?"

91. "How could you ever know how I feel, when you have never been through what I have?"

Unless this question is attended to nondefensively, your credibility with your client may be jeopardized. Clients who have been harshly abused are especially likely to fling this curve ball at you as a challenge to your ability to define your problem-solving skills and resources. One doesn't "have to have been there" to be of good service. The mistaken notion that you either have to be one to understand one (e.g., abuse survivor) or have been there, (e.g., a traumatic experience) to be a legitimate supplier of helping services can be countered with these ideas:

- "Because I believe you when you tell me how you feel."
- "Have there been times in your life when although you never experienced what someone else did, you still had a very good ball park estimate as to how that individual felt?"
- "Does a surgeon have to have had open heart surgery to have a sense for what his patient is feeling?"
- "Some people are just naturally pretty good at understanding the feelings of others, regardless of whether they had the same experience themselves."
- "Try me."
- "Humans have common feelings even though they may not have unusual experiences in common."
- "If I felt emotionally hurt about something that happened to me, could you understand how I felt even though the same thing had not happened to you?"
- "Perhaps I couldn't easily hit the bull's-eye of understanding, but I bet I could come close to it."
- "Will a partial understanding do?"
- "Because I couldn't completely understand you doesn't mean I would have no compassion at all for your emotions or that I could not be of assistance in any way."

92. "I must treat (do unto) others just as I would like them to treat (do unto) me."
    This golden rule overlooks individual differences. One size doesn't fit all regarding how others would like to be treated and to insist that one must treat others as you would like to be treated is to display self-centeredness.

Rewording this statement to "it would be better for me to treat (do unto) others as they would prefer me to treat (do unto) them" gives fairer consideration to people not being clones of one another concerning their preferred way of your treatment of them. The following alternative messages can help to highlight flexibility and individual distinctiveness when determining what would be the better method of treating another:

- "Oh, aren't you really saying that everyone wants to be treated just like you do?"
- "How does this idea fit the notion that humans are infinitely variable?"
- "Is this idea given in the form of a commandment or a recommendation?"
- "What do you think—if others truly treated others the way they would like to be treated, would there be less or fewer misunderstandings?"
- "Let's suppose that someone isn't just like you, in fact is extremely different from you. How would this proposal fit for them?"
- "Then are one and all required to buy into the way that you would like to be treated?"
- "Do you think people are more one- or multi-dimensional?"
- "What about those mavericks whose poison is your meat. What is one to do with them?"
- "By your logic you would then end up treating individuals who are different, all the same."

93. "When I do so many good things for others, what is so wrong about expecting something in return?"
   One hand washes the other—oh, really? Often others will sit idly back and gladly allow you to do their work for them—and not lift a finger in returning even a part of your favor! Teaching clients the value of developing a philosophy of nonreciprocation, making themselves less reinforceable, is a valuable lesson in that it makes them less beholden to others. Distinguishing between hoping for reward and recognition without making them essential provides a realistic view

of expectations of others by way of their tracking, appreciating, and returning your efforts on their behalf. Better that clients be encouraged to make provisions for other reasons intrinsic to themselves, e.g., that they find value to pitching in and offering their assistance, rather than for an extrinsic payoff provided by the benefactor of their good works. The following comments, questions, and statements are designed to squelch the rumor that one good turn after another deserves at least something in return:

- "Because happiness is a direct ratio between what you expect and what you get, and if reality throws cold water in your face in the form of no return on your investment, you may end up making yourself feel dismayed."
- "This type of scorekeeping breeds sulking and self-pity. What do you think about what I'm saying?"
- "Often when people use the words 'expect something in return' they really mean 'demand something in return.' Which is it for you?"
- "Expecting less may numb some of the disappointment, or worse yet, anguish that stems from your overreaction to others' decision to leave you high and dry by way of not boomeranging back to you a return on your offerings."
- "Because humans often motivate themselves by the philosophies of '50/50—50 you give and 50 I take' and 'you for me—and me for me.'"
- "By expecting others not to do what they often do by way of take-for-grantedness and one-sidedness, you're setting yourself up to feel how?"
- "What is wrong is what defeats your self-interest; is expecting others to deliver the goods just because you do in or against your best interest?"
- "It's only wrong if it hurts a human being, including yourself—where does it get you to have high expectations that people are going to be at least partially as generous in their giving as you?"

94. "I would never even think of treating them the way they treat me."

The implication here is that others don't have the right to be different in their conduct toward you as it opposes yours toward them. Putting your values center stage without tolerantly differentiating them from others' often results in a rude awakening when your idea scheme is betrayed, as it inevitably will be. Catastrophic thinking, e.g., "How horrible that I am made to suffer such neglect and abuse from others. What awful thing did I do to deserve such retaliation" is often evoked when others do not treat you as you have treated them. This rather self-centered view should be replaced with more tolerant philosophies that allow for individual differences in conveying respect and kindness. Influencing clients' acceptance of treatment that contrasts with their own relationship sustaining methods include:

- "Is there a law of the universe that is violated when someone's behavior toward you is remarkably contrasted to yours toward them?"
- "Can others think differently from you—can this person?"
- "Are others entitled to their or to your thoughts?"
- "Given such a reality of differences in treatment, what conclusion would be in your best interests?"
- "Would it be fair and democratic if others were mandated to treat you as you treat them?"
- "Would it be better to conclude that others are entitled to self-determine their treatment of you?"
- "Why must others borrow a page from your book, or more to the point, go by your etiquette book?"
- "Now that they have violated your interpersonal sanctions, what would be an emotionally healthy way to look at that fact?"

95. "When I feel happy, why can't it last?"
    Happiness is difficult to sustain and this fact is often even more difficult to accept. If not taught otherwise, the ongoing happiness solution can be transposed into a problem, e.g., "I *have to* be more continually happy," since perhaps the least likely way to be more consistently happy is to insist that you be so. Demanding "I should/must/have to be happier" will worsen the ability to ex-

tend this enjoyable state of mind. Clients can be encouraged to take pressure off themselves to achieve longer-lasting happiness using these points and counterpoints:

- "Apparently you don't have the capacity for chronic happiness."
- "Because in part happiness is due to circumstances beyond your control."
- "Because sustaining can be harder than gaining."
- "With a basis for comparison, you can better appreciate those contrasting, not so happy moments."
- "The law of averages in practically any project is going to fall in the middle range, including project happiness."
- "The feature of happiness is like any other when put on a bell-shaped curve; a few people are either happy or unhappy much of the time, with the large majority falling someplace in the middle."
- "Simply because the conditions of life often don't last long enough to convenience feeling happy."
- "As far as is known, nothing is forever."
- "Because of the many curve balls life throws you, it is likely that you will strike out on at least some of them."

96. "Why do others have to make such a big deal out of it?" Nothing is so small that at least some, often a majority of people can't blow it out of proportion. Humans respond differently and unpredictably to the same event. What one might see as catastrophic another might view as opportunity. The emotional reaction to a life circumstance is often highly correlated with whether one is asking or giving. Clients should be instructed to realize that others will often respond to them and their situation in a more emotionally charged way than what they would desire. Otherwise, they will continue to make themselves feel aghast about others' unusual (to them) manner of response. The following commentary attempts to enlist more acceptance and respect for such incomprehensible response by others:

- "Do humans ever respond the same way to the same circumstance?"
- "Because this is one of the things that humans do best–give themselves a flair for the insignificant."
- "By choice."
- "Because some find it difficult to not rattle their own cage."
- "Maybe in their own way they just want to make sure that they are heard."
- "Whose prerogative do you think it is to express these various emotions?"
- "Do others have to have a special reason for doing so?"
- "Because that is apparently their way."
- "What reason would prove acceptable from your standpoint?"

97. "Who says they have a right to act like this?"
    This question implies that there is a captain who addresses the alleged inquiry of 'May I act in ways that meet your blessing?'" The original question as well as the presumed crew leader, defies the principle of free will. Fact: Humans willingly and repeatedly will act badly, and require no special reason for doing so. This inquiry is often meant to really say "I didn't say that they have a right to act this way, and until I do they must not!" This hidden demand for "my will not free will" had best be identified and challenged and can be done by using such persuasions as follows:

- "Where is special permission to be gained?"
- "Is there really a unique entitlement to be found that is essential for individual expression?"
- "Who is on the list of possibilities for the 'who' of 'who says'?"
- "Do you think that there has to be some sort of divine approval at work here?"
- "The nature of the beast, that's who."
- "Free will overriding your will."
- "Perhaps whoever runs the universe can take responsibility."
- "What would you do if you ever found out who 'who' is?"

98.   "They should know that I didn't mean anything by it."
      "Read my bloody mind's intentions and my even more
      bloody methods in a way that accepts minimal attempt on
      my part to do wrong" is the message of this proclamation.
      The idea that others should be able to cut through the smoke
      to determine if there is a fire reflects the self-centered idea
      that others are obligated to find what wavelength the client
      is on, and then get themselves on the same dial tone–and
      that how to accomplish such a mind-reading feat is others'
      responsibility to figure out. The client would do well to
      realize that others will naturally know less about his inten-
      tions than he does. This paves the way for treating others
      more accommodatingly in the service of better relationship
      upkeep. Ideas that foster more diplomacy and less demand
      upon others to be privy to one's apparent good intentions
      include:

- "How can others know what you know if you don't tell them?"
- "How do you know things about others when they don't tell
  you?"
- "What was it about your behavior that they said led them to
  their conclusions?"
- "If they could read the intentions of your mind they could get
  rich in the stock market."
- "Whose responsibility is it to define intentions?"
- "Aren't you really demanding something of them by way of
  knowledge that only you can give them?"
- "Where does this insistence ultimately get you?"
- "Are the misunderstandings worth the refusals to explain your
  intentions?"

99.   "They should know they are making me feel bad."
      These double-barreled faulty irrational ideas will likely lead
      to anger and retaliation unless smoked and snuffed out.
      Demanding that others become mind readers while presum-
      ing that they are the cause of one's upset detracts from
      taking better charge of one's emotional well-being. Others
      are often not aware of one's emotional response to them–
      and couldn't care less as to what it is. Demands for an

emotional wavelength coupled with blaming others for inner turmoil can be prevented with these altering responses:

- "How does one go about reading another's mind?"
- "How does one go about giving or transplanting an emotion inside you?"
- "Why must others strongly consider their influence on you?"
- "If they can't make you happier, how can they make you miserable?"
- "Why must they change before you can feel better?"
- "Is it fair and realistic to expect others to be able to read your bloody mind?"
- "How does one go about the business of making another feel bad?"
- "What is to prevent you from making others aware of your feelings about their behavior?"
- "Must others be aware of your emotions as well as better accommodate them?"

100. "After knowing me for so long, you would think he/she would know what I want and don't want. Don't you agree?"
   Clients who have relationship problems will try to draw you into aligning with their "rightness" and their associates' "wrongness." With you implanted in the middle as an ally, an individual can maneuver himself into a position of "good guy" versus "bad guy." Support for this mind-reading/fingerpointing perspective can be withdrawn so that more problem-solution methods can be employed. The following rejoinders can avoid this taking-sides entrapment:

- "If you were your partner, would you be able to know what you wanted?"
- "Let's say I did agree, how would that prove your position correct?"
- "What sort of fallout could come from your insistence that your associates have never-ending correct assumptions about your wants?"

- "If I agreed with your associate as you're asking me to agree with you, what would you conclude about my therapy methods?"
- "Would it be better to ask for what you want or to wait until your mate knows you well enough to see through to your brain?"
- "Do you want me to say what I think on this matter or what I think you think and want me to think and say?"
- "Sign language aside, how does one go about identifying another's wishes without asking?"
- "How might too much agreement by me with one or the other of you not be good for our problem-solving purposes?"

101. "Who do you think is more in the right and more in the wrong on this matter?"
      This scorekeeping question identifies you as judge and jury rather than as helper. Courtroom festivities would be well to be avoided lest the solution-finding purposes get lost in the who's-to-blame shuffle. Redirecting the interviewing process toward finding remedies rather than fault can be done with some of the following directives:

- "Is our goal here to pin fault and blame on each other or to solve problems?"
- "I think the main culprit is the emotional disturbance you each create within yourself and who has created more of it. Well, sometimes it seems like a horse apiece."
- "What I might see as an imbalance, someone else might not."
- "Do you think that finding out is essential for our purposes?"
- "I think that would largely depend on what day of the week it was–and at that time the one of you is probably making himself/herself so upset he/she can't remember which day it is!"
- "Are you more interested in playing detective and looking for evidence to defend yourself or determining how you can do better in the future?"
- "In what ways do you honestly think that my opinion would be important for you?"

102. "How could anyone not, and who wouldn't, blame them-
      selves after what I did?"
      Is there such an animal as an unforgiven sin? Permissive
      philosophies that render emotional slack are favored in
      rational problem solving in that they permit a more clear-
      headed outlook, reducing the chances of committing fu-
      ture errors. Until self-forgiveness and self-acceptance for
      and in spite of past blunders are firmly established, prob-
      lem-solving efforts will likely come to a screeching halt.
      The self-blame hatchet can be set aside by use of the
      following encouraging counters:

- "Who wouldn't blame themselves after a wicked deed—somebody in their right mind, that's who!"
- "How could anyone not blame themselves following such a
  putrid act? By *vigorously* self-stating 'That was mighty foolish
  of me, but I'm not an almighty fool.'"
- "Someone who wanted to suffer less would not blame themselves."
- "Simply applying heavy doses of compassion in the aftermath
  of a mistake will prevent self-blame."
- "Someone who chose to not act immorally, meaning not to
  hurt themselves with self-damnation, would not blame themselves."
- "Someone who had all their tolerant marbles could and would
  not choose to blame themselves in the aftermath of even their
  most foolish error."
- "Someone who wanted to put their stubbornness to good use
  by staunchly refusing to blame themselves for whatever hid-
  eous act they committed."

103. "How could I possibly stand it if the worst happened?"
      A client recently stated, "I can't stand living!" Wonder-
      ing if she might be suicidal, I asked, "Do you have any
      thoughts of harming yourself?" She replied, "Oh no, I
      can't stand the idea of dying!" Whether in life or death,
      war or peace, prosperity or poverty, humans tend to exag-
      gerate how difficult it is to tolerate something. "I-can't-
      stand-it-itis" is one of the major maladies of the human

condition and can be countered and debated by some of the following response selections:

- "To say you can't stand something implies that you will die from that activity or association, and if that would happen we would give you a decent burial (at least that is what we tell you now)."
- "What would you ask yourself to tolerate that hasn't been stomached before?"
- "By digging in your heels and refusing to leave the situation until you turn the corner."
- "You could start to stand it by getting started in doing so."
- "By understanding that those who give up their comfort by facing the worst experience more comfort."
- "By accepting whatever the worst might be."
- "You could focus more on the long-range comforts of holding your ground rather than the short-range discomfort of attending to the matter."
- "By seeing that what you say you 'can't stand' doesn't have to go away before you can feel better."

104. "Can you help me to become a better person?"
It takes a month of Sundays if not an eternity to find something that doesn't exist–including human worth. Many problems of this earth are those of self-proving, and it would be important to not go on a journey that has no destination. To teach clients how they can secure more advantages for themselves so that they will be better off in their existence is the essence of good therapy. To allow them to conclude without rebuttal that they are better people due to their being better off is about the closest you can get to a crime without actually committing one. Avoid going along with the gag of the "rating game" whereby one gives oneself a report card with a good mark for some external prop such as a high-tech performance or for being among the very popular. This is an outstanding achievement in that it heads off at the pass clients' tendencies to put themselves at the mercy of their successes and others' acclaim. Driving this humanistic

point across at a time when clients strive for superhumanness can be accomplished with the following rational redirections:

- "What constitutes the requirements of a 'better person'?"
- "Do you think there is a distinction between being better off and being a better person?"
- "I'm afraid I can't help you to find something that doesn't exist, like being a better person. Let me explain."
- "Do you think there is any evidence that your advantages equal you?"
- "Where is the proof that your disadvantages represent you?"
- "If someone I know is better off than me, does that make that person better than me?"
- "I think I can help you to help yourself to accept yourself and to perhaps be better off, but I'm afraid that I can't get you into the kingdom of heaven."
- "I think I can help you to help yourself uplift your emotions but not to uplift your personhood."
- "I think I can help you to dissolve your emotional interferences, which will make it more likely that you will be more clearheadedly able to do your own bidding, but I can't grant you nobility."
- "I believe you can learn to better appreciate your value to yourself and your ability to enjoy life, but not to establish or increase your value or worth."

105. "Maybe if I get angry enough others will listen to me."
Anger is anti-collaborative and against mutual understanding. Emotional drama may get another's attention, but it will likely be drawn toward the wrong thing—the emotional outburst itself to the neglect of the message behind the theatrics. Anger fogs understanding and is a poor communication tool. If direct, forthright messages are not heeded it is unlikely that hostile, angry communications will be. Anger will take poor communication outcomes and make them worse. Discourage clients from

experiencing self-defeat by trying to accelerate their message via anger through the following points of discussion:

- "How will angrily trying to do others in encourage them to hear what you have to say?"
- "Can you think of other ways to get a message across short of seeing red?"
- "Think, has others' anger at you resulted in your being more or less receptive to their message?"
- "How can a porcupine influence his social group?"
- "What are some better methods of communication minus the anger?"
- "Does one ordinarily catch more flies with honey or vinegar?"
- "What do you think would be some of the fallout from your switching gears to anger?"
- "If anger is so good, why does it feel so bad?"
- "What does history tell us about the effects anger has on people better understanding one another?"
- "Is it a dire necessity to gain and maintain another's listening ear?"
- "Why is it so almighty important that you be listened to?"
- "Your anger at best might encourage others to *pretend* to listen to you, but would it really support a more legitimate effort?"

106.   "Once I start doing the wrong thing, why can't I stop?" Taking a bad situation and making it worse seems like such a convenience item. Putting a foot on the brakes rather than the gas pedal following a mistake is difficult even from a scientific standpoint, e.g., the principle of inertia says an object going in a given direction tends to propel itself by its own momentum. Added emotional fortitude is ordinarily required to prevent this principle from being allowed to become an overriding factor. Educating clients to distinguish between a slip and a major setback can be the salvation of self-destruction. Due to human imperfection it is not a question of if the individual is going to push him/herself off the wagon of a self-help program but when, how severely, and the length of

the individual's slip. A relapse-prevention program can help to set boundaries on the frequency, intensity, and duration of cognitive, emotive, and behavioral backsliding. The following directives can be of assistance in de-escalating frequent tendencies to extend rather than disband human error:

- "Overreaction to the original mistake can assist you to prompt an extension of your blunder."
- "Judging yourself by the original negative outcome often implies a promise to yourself to continue to forge ahead badly in light of your conclusion that you are a bad person."
- "Because you haven't learned from your mistake."
- "It's not that you 'can't,' it's just that you may not have learned how to yet."
- "Don't pretend to not know what you do know, and think back to a time when you were successful in better regulating your original fault, and how you managed to do so."
- "What are some ways that you think you could help yourself in the future to not create a multiplying effect following a mistake?"
- "Try to lessen whatever tendencies you have to exaggerate the significance of your beginning deficiency and see if that doesn't douse rather than fan the flames of your concern."
- "Because you neglect to tell yourself such things as 'don't throw gasoline on this mistake,' 'cool your jets,' 'it's not the end of the world,' 'because I make a mistake doesn't mean that I have to keep making it,' 'lighten up,' and 'although the world isn't going to come to an end due to my mistake–if I keep making it I will needlessly pyramid further disadvantages.'"
- "Just as you started by getting started, you can stop by stopping yourself."
- "I think when you clearly understand and accept that there is no magic to stopping and that nothing stops you but you stopping you, you will be better able to do so."
- "Try to better appreciate that restraint, even after lack of restraint, is not a dirty word."

107. "How can I teach him/her a lesson that won't soon be forgotten?"

This pointed question implies that its holder has a streak of anger, vindictiveness, and resentment wrapped up in it. George Orwell rightly defined revenge as "a childish daydream." Two wrongs don't make a right and it would be better to discourage clients from a punitive, almighty stance toward the wrongdoer. Otherwise, an escalation of feuding and conflict is likely to transpire from such take-it-upon-oneself teachings. Aggressiveness can be discouraged and tolerance and more civilized alternative methods of raising the consciousness of contrary-acting others can be encouraged by the following eye-opening suggestions and persuasions:

- "What good would it do you to have a wounded animal for an associate?"
- "Think of times that you have been harshly penalized in the past. How was your character helped by and what were your feelings toward your penalizers?"
- "Is it really possible to teach someone a lesson that they don't want to learn?"
- "Are you taking this mandate upon yourself or has some higher authority ordained you to do so?"
- "Do you think it will be more the punishment or the lesson that they will be more likely to forget to remember to forget?"
- "Are your teachings more designed to help the other or for you to give vent to your animosity?"
- "What do you think your chances are of forcefully transplanting a different value system into another's head?"

108. "How come I always skip around (when I try to understand and overcome my problems)?"

Gaining and maintaining clients' attention can be a difficult task. Due to their emotional discomforts as well as their easily distractable nature they will look around the room, around their problems, and in other inattentive ways make themselves to be in the session, but not of the session. Often aware of their lack of focus they try to analyze it to the neglect of undoing their hit-and-miss, search-and-destroy approach to problem solving. They are often reluctant to discontinue this seat-of-the-pants pattern because if they did they might tempt themselves to expend the energy required to track a specific goal. Motivation by the excitement and intrigue of whimsically moving about in conversation, the immediate conve nience gained from not forcefully focusing on a particu- lar task, seemingly avoiding failure by not trying at any one thing in particular, and low frustration tolerance ten- dencies that dramatize the strain involved in attempting concentrated success are frequently the rules rather than the exceptions. Clients' awareness of and their yen to analyze their scattered-thinking resistances is not enough to prompt a change in the therapeutic weather toward more precise, sustained goals. Getting past this once- over-lightly approach to problem solving is more likely to be accomplished with the following rational instiga- tions that encourage clients to unblock themselves from why-and-wherefore irrelevancies:

- "If you didn't skip around what would you more likely require yourself to do?"
- "Instead of 'Why do I skip around?' wouldn't it be better to ask yourself 'What are the consequences of my fickleness in problem solving?' and try to learn from those aftereffects?"
- "Perhaps you find the preliminaries more exciting than the main event."
- "Let's figure out how you actively encourage yourself to pro- mote such checkered mannerisms."
- "Analysis is fun and games; changing up-until-now-hit-and- miss patterns is work. Do you want to feel better right now by looking for needles in haystacks that may not exist—or do you want to feel better for the rest of your life by prioritizing and bearing down on precise goals?"
- "I can either be nice to you by searching for alleged special reasons for your flighty ways, or I can try to help you by insist-

ing that you get yourself down to brass tacks while carving out a philosophy of sustained effort for yourself."
- " 'Always' sounds hopeless and fatalistic. Would there be a more hopeful way to describe what you're up against?"
- "What, by your view, happens to a person who flutters through problem solving? How is this person's life likely to turn out?"

109. "Why can't I ever get anything done on time?"
Ongoing explanations for chronic tardiness don't assist in the early bird getting the worm. Yet, latecomers continue to search for packaged understandings for their foot dragging. It doesn't seem to dawn on them that no reason for this nonchalance is going to replace their "putting off until tomorrow what has been put off until today" philosophy. Only their own good intentions backed by the right methods can do that. Rattling clients' cages and time clocks while persuading them to get themselves up to speed can be afforded by the following insinuations and declarations:

- "Because you see to it that the price isn't right—instead try giving yourself some negative consequences for your lack of disciplined planning."
- "Perhaps you're too stubborn to take a serious look at meeting the requirements of overcoming your noncompliance in better living within your time constraints."
- "Is it that you 'can't' get things done on time, or that you 'won't' do so?"
- "Because it appears easier to preach a sermon with your lips, rather than with your life."
- "Because you actively encourage yourself not to. Now how might you be doing that?"
- "Because you take one or more pause(s) too many along the way."
- "It may be that you believe because you 'never' get things done on time that its unlikely that you 'ever' will."

- "Oftentimes people sacredize the inconvenience of meeting the requirements of timeliness. Are you?"

110. "What is it going to take to succeed?"
     Whether a person has the resources to succeed cannot be known until after available expenditures have been spent. When clients request a surefire formula for success it is important not to discourage their yearnings for accomplishment, yet temper such hopefulness with realistic uncertainty—you never really know for sure. This balance of encouragement spiked with realism can be seen in the following rational propositions:

- "Success."
- "Knowing tomorrow's requirements for success today can leave Jack a dull boy."
- "Getting a data base from your hypothesis about a given project can help to point you in the general direction of success in the future."
- "Wanting likelihood for success makes life interesting, motivating, and realistic; insistences for success make it stressful, discouraging, and fantasy-filled."
- "You will know for sure if and when you get there."
- "Play the odds while using the chance factor to work against any dire need for certainty—in an uncertain world."
- "Discovering the right ingredients as you fail along the way."
- "By failing enough times to do what's right and applying those learnings in the next chapter."
- "Probably a lot of search and researching."
- "Convincing yourself that failure isn't bigger than life and the worst of all possible crimes."
- "Accepting that the most successful people fail the most."

111. "I've tried that all (everything that you suggested) before, and it didn't work."
     Forcefully making the distinction between sustained and unsustained effort is a part of psychotherapy that often goes unattended. Trying a lot of things for a little while doesn't provide an accurate measurement of the effec-

tiveness of any one strategy. This statement implies that you are expected to fill in the missing pieces when there may be none; the more difficult the life circumstances and the more modes of helping tried, the greater likelihood that it is not so much a matter of discovering missing pieces to the problem-solving puzzle, but rather repeatedly using those parts already in hand. Inviting clients to persist and not resist in getting data from repeated observations and outcomes of more concentrated efforts can be accomplished with some of these suggestive rebuttals:

- "If at first you don't succeed, try and try again."
- "What did you learn from your failings that you can apply in future go-arounds?"
- "What do you think Mark Twain meant when he said, 'It takes me three weeks to prepare for an impromptu speech'?"
- "Is it that 'it' doesn't work or that you haven't been yet able to make it work?"
- "Do you think it's more that ideas will work for you, or that you will (repeatedly) work for them?"
- "Have you tried any of these 'losing' formulas over a period of time?"
- "Would you be willing to try one or two of the more hopeful multiple selections already tried for a longer period of time to see what data reading is produced?"

112. "But how do you change your thinking?"
      The "how to's" of uprooting mistaken philosophies of life are preferably examined within the context of the clients' motivation to realign their thinking. Few will opt for change until they clearly understand that it is in their best interest to do so. Persuasion and salespersonship by the therapist are often necessary elements for fortifying incentive. Getting the client to be convinced and then to in turn convince you of the value of attitudinal change is an ultimate therapeutic endeavor. The following questions and directives are designed to get at the mechanics

of alternative thinking while first identifying good reasons for doing so:

- "Itemizing reasons why it is to your advantage to change would be a good start."
- "What are some examples of experiences that you have had that illustrate that it's time for a cool change in your thinking?"
- "*But* how do you do it? Mainly by getting off your butt."
- "The best way to change an irrational thought is to act against it. What is an example of an action you can take before the day is out that would begin to tear away at an irrational notion?"
- "What things have been a source of motivating yourself to change your thinking in the past?"
- "Scrutinize the credentials for their validity; become your own best scientist by asking yourself about what you believe to be true, 'Where is the evidence for the accuracy of what I believe?'—push for substantiation, proof, logic."
- "Acclimate yourself to and accept the discomfort that often accompanies change; don't startle and intimidate yourself by its awkwardness."
- "By your willingness to engage in exercising your free will in seeing and acting upon the idea that anything you believe, you can also disbelieve."
- "Building emotional muscle contains the same principles as building physical muscle—practice, drill, repetition. Exercise the weaker ideas you wish to strengthen and don't exercise the notions that you wish to weaken."

113. "What if I've never done that before?"
   A script that humans often invent is "If something has not occurred or been made to happen up until now—e.g., success, a new venture—it cannot be made to happen in the future." This restrictive notion is yet another example of convenient thinking. After all, if I believe that if I never have and never will accomplish something, then I smugly and comfortably don't have to bother to lift a finger in effort. This ominous inquiry hints at this sit-on-your-hands mentality. It is almost as if a statute of limita-

tions has been declared beyond which change cannot take place. Uninventing this loaded question with all its avoidance insinuations can be tackled with the following persuasions:

- "So, what if?"
- "As far as I know there is no universal statute of limitations beyond which change cannot take place."
- "You can expect a decent burial if you die trying (I think)."
- "Then you can entertain the possibility of the excitement of a new experience."
- "What are you waiting for?"
- "Does because you have never done something before mean that you can't touch base with it now?"
- "Perhaps, up until now you haven't left room for the possibility of change in that area. What do you think?"
- "Then that's one less mountain–or molehill–you have not yet climbed."

114.   "If I like something, why can't I have it?"
Another script invention is "If I find somebody or something to my liking–then I need same." This question posed by clients longingly implies that when one sees a resource it seems natural that one must have immediate access to it. It would be better to squelch such fairy-tale thinking in favor of more realistic, nondemanding views. Combining desires, preferences, and wishes into necessities is where sanity leaves off and emotional disturbance begins. Rerouting such false, flaming idealisms can be directed by these more elastic suggestions:

- "Because you get what you get, not what you want."
- "Maybe it's not in the cards."
- "Perhaps there is not enough to go around for everyone who wants it."
- "Could be that you haven't met the requirements of earning it."
- "Might be that someone wants it more."
- "Others might have better access to it."

- "Due to your limitations in overcoming the necessary obstacles to gain it."
- "There may be no special reasons, only unspecified ones."
- "In some cases too much time and not enough money; in other cases too much money and not enough time."

115.   "When I don't like something, why do I have to get it or have it happen?"
    The grandiose idea that bad things should only happen to the other guy is reflected in this whiny question. Whether one is decent-acting or not is beside the point; no one is immune from adversity, yet this inquiry implies that it must be otherwise. The weight of this not-so-silent prayer for inoculation from hassle can be lifted by use of these counters and confrontations:

- "Because sometimes you are at the wrong place at the wrong time."
- "Since life is for lessons, and since you likely will learn more from adversity than from success, one of the purposes of life is fulfilled through your misfortune."
- "Must only favorable happenings occur in your life?"
- "Because you just happen to be standing in the way."
- "Sometimes due to your deficiencies in avoiding happenings that you find distasteful."
- "Because you're either living wrong, right, or someplace in between."
- "Because circumstances often come together to produce selection against you."
- "Because you didn't get to the pass in time to head off the misfortune."

116.   "But I was always taught this way."
    "I must follow my upbringing" is the declaration behind this phrase with a nostalgic ring to it. Putting on the blinders has some immediate reinforcers; you don't have to expend the energy to think, you escape disapproval, you don't have to put yourself through the discomforts associated with reexamining and, heaven forbid, revamp-

ing your values; you will feel cozy, your original teachers will approve, and you can bask in the sedentary state of business per usual. Getting clients past their reluctance to uproot long-standing irrational ideas requires a fair amount of jostling and therapeutic anarchy. Direct confrontation and convincing of the merits of reshuffling their values to see if they can deal themselves a better hand can be spelled out with the following notations:

- "Were you taught or did you learn and then keep alive original teachings?"
- "If you were told now for the first time, would you believe it?"
- "If you were taught that lice made good eating, would you be required to still believe it?"
- "Would there be advantages to making yourself less teachable in the present?"
- "What is more important, what was spelled out for you way back when or what you believe now?"
- "If you believe yourself to be stuck in the bowels of your past understandings, do you wish to get yourself unstuck?"
- "Is it more in your best interests to believe the way you choose to or the way others have thought you 'should'?"
- "What would be some advantages to your contradicting some of your from-the-beginning-of-time ideas?"
- "Is it possible that you had good teachers with bad messages?"
- "Can you tell me one exception to the rule, a major original belief that you have given up, and how you managed to do it?"
- "Do you believe in free will in the form of anything you have learned and believe, you can unlearn and disbelieve?"

117. "I'm not going to get mad—just get even."
      Vengefulness, vindictiveness, and unforgivingness are written all over this different yet similar intention. Stubbornly refusing to abandon the hostility it is couched in leaves its holder with the burden of stalking an opportunity to vent this aggressive notion. One of the best ways to stay out of harm's way is to not harm others. What benefit is it, and of what pleasure is it, to be associated

with a wounded animal? Discouraging clients antagonisms can be assisted with these distinctions and dictums:

- "Are you sure you're not talking about one and the same?"
- "Is it possible that by getting even you may win the battle but lose the war against emotional disturbance?"
- "What crowning glory can be found by crowning your associate?"
- "Could this be the same hearse (with your name on it) with a different license plate?"
- "All things considered and in the long run, are the consequences of revenge more sweet or more bitter?"
- "What will it profit a person to harm another with a cactus, if in the end his hands are bloody?"
- "Rather than 'get even,' why not do yourself an even bigger favor by leaving your guns and mean-spirited schemes at home?"
- "Is not your get-even mentality simply another song-and-dance version of "an eye for an eye and a tooth for a tooth"—with a lot of blind, toothless people walking around—scripture?"

118. "How can I get my needs met?"

Emotional reeducation begins right here! Until you can get clients to abolish alleged human needs they will likely remain emotionally cooked. Even survival is not a need; it is a choice. Emphasis upon "I need this, that, or the other thing" creates a cringe in the gut that expresses the fear of going without or losing presumed needs. Love, approval, cooperation, understanding, encouragement, affirmation, achievement, and other personal and interpersonal niceties are just that—very nice, but not necessities. Needy people are desperate, fearful, controlling, angry people whose overriding goal in life is to cover you like a blanket so that you can provide them with what they demand from you. People who need people are the most miserable people in the world, bottomless emotional pits who fuse with you tightly in hopes that you won't discontinue your endless provisions. In the long run they drive others away and defeat their own purposes by their endless enmeshment. One of the biggest favors you can do for a client is to try to argue her out of the idea that she has needs that absolutely must be met if she is to achieve any semblance of happiness. The following divergent, if not argumentative, views can be a takeoff for rational disputations geared at getting a client to give herself some emotional slack by urging herself to cast aside this "neediness":

- "When you tell yourself that you absolutely 'need' something how do you honestly make yourself feel?"
- "Let's pretend that I believe that I need certain things from others, such as love and approval, or that I need or have to do a certain thing such as perform or achieve exceptionally if not perfectly well. Why and how might you want to talk me out of such presumed requirements?"
- "What does the idea 'You don't need anything in life, not even to survive; you choose to do such things' mean for you?"
- "Do you know any 'needy' people? What is it like to be around them?"
- "If you can't think of any 'needy' people, what do you think it would be like to be around such dependent folks?"
- "How might proclaiming and insisting for a solution that would meet your 'needs' create more problems?"
- "What do you think is meant by 'one of the main causes of problems are needy solutions'?"
- "What does the idea 'Thinking that you need something will give you a bad case of white knuckles, mean for you?"
- "How might hanging on for dear life to your seeming 'needs' contribute to the emotional death of you?"
- "Do you think there is a contrast in feelings when you self-state 'I want, would like, prefer certain favors from others and accomplishments in life' versus 'I absolutely need, require, have to have certain essentials'?"

119. "I'm entitled to better treatment than that!"
      Entitlements are really figments that are either invisible or nonexistent. In either case they do not constitute assets

that can be counted on. Demands for entitlements often mask the God-almighty philosophy of "Everybody is entitled to my values generally and my opinion on this topic specifically." This childish daydream implies that one is anointed to automatically be the benefactor of certain resources simply because one exists. Self-styled entitlements also imply that the beholder of such treasures is a "special" person. However, humans aren't special–they are unique. Being unique is nothing to sneeze at. However, the fact that there is nobody else on this green earth like you does not allot you any "special" privileges.

When people demand their absentee entitlements they are presuming that they are "special" and consequently are likely to hold at least three false, self-defeating expectations as an offshoot of their grandiose, king- or queen-of-the-hill assumption; these are: (1) "Because I'm so special, I must/have to forever and always give special performances and make favorable impressions; after all, special people like me have to leave behind a success-filled legacy." (2) "Because I'm so special others must/have to treat me special; after all, nobility and rank have their privileges." (3) "Because I'm so special, life and the universe must/have to grant me special favors so that each and every time I seek, I can very easily and quickly obtain what I strive for." Suggesting that clients set aside these immature fantasies en route to reaping the benefits, such as minimizing self-indulgence generally and self-pity specifically, can be done by interjecting some of the following commentary:

- "What do you think is the difference between telling yourself 'give me a break' and your believing 'I create my own breaks'?"
- "How much room do you think there would be on the top if everyone who thought they actually had advantages coming, got them?"
- "How does thinking (about entitlements) make it so?"

- "What argument might you have with the notion that you get what you get in life—not what you presume you're entitled to?"
- "In your opinion what are some disadvantages to your entitlement theory?"
- "What do you think would happen if two or more people strongly believed that they were entitled to the same thing at the same time?"
- "Must others provide you with the kind of favorable treatment you identify as being owed you?"
- "Because you insistently ask, must others provide?"
- "Have there ever been times when you didn't get what you thought you were entitled to—and were happier than a lark that you didn't?"

120. "How can I stop him/her from emotionally destroying me?"

The seeds of emotional "destruction" are planted with the cooperation of the "destructee." The false premise behind this fatalistic question implies the questioner to be a sitting duck for another's wrath and harsh criticism. Looking at the conduct of others as causing one's upset discourages self-initiative. After all, if someone is causing the client disturbance that person must change before the client can get out from underneath his/her emotional upheaval. Provide to the client ideas that correct his notion that someone else is administering to him heavy doses of emotional devastation. Instead, bring attention to the relationship reality that it takes two to tango—one to lead with unpleasant conduct and the other to follow by overreacting to displeasing tactics. Corrective ideas include:

- "By changing your tune and seeing, understanding, and accepting that although others influence you, you upset yourself."
- "What do you think the idea 'You have met the enemy and the enemy is you' means?"
- "How does the idea 'Nobody can emotionally destroy you without your authorization,' hit you?"

- "If you can't stop the negative stimulus then you might want to consider stopping the destructive response."
- "How do you think others are able to escape emotional destruction given similar circumstances as you describe?"
- "During the times you think, feel, and behave in ways that better cushion the irritant, what in your own words do you do differently?"
- "Talk with people who don't seem to get themselves as flustered as you given similar circumstances, and see if you can uncover some of the tricks of the trade."
- "Try not judging yourself or others by their ill-advised conduct toward you along with not exaggerating the significance of either their inability to treat you more favorably or your inability to cope more favorably with those who seem to come at you as if they were hornets leaving a nest."

121. "There has got to be a solution to all of this."
     Preparing the client for the reality that behind every storm cloud there isn't a silver lining and that therefore the solution to some problems is to accept the fact that there may not be any, is no fun. Yet, reality-based emotional reeducation had best have as its platform a touching of all problem-solving bases. Getting the client to accept the grim (but not too grim) reality that due to an imperfect world inhabited by–you guessed it–imperfect people, any or all solutions to a problem may turn out to be null and void, reflects this encompassing philosophy. If no problem-solving-stone possibility is to be left unturned it would be fitting that clients be informed that solving a presenting problem may or may not be in the cards. That way, pressure can be taken off the problem-solving venture because the solution is no longer seen as all-important. Also, less disappointment is likely to stem from not putting all of one's eggs into the solution-finding basket. Counter thoughts that desacredize a discovery of a solution include:

- "What does the 'got to' do to your stress level?"

- "It's good that you desire a solution, but why must there be one?"
- "What do you think ordinarily occurs when a person takes the possibility of a solution out of a life-or-death context?"
- "How does commanding a solution help you to find one?"
- "Have there been other times in your life that you insisted upon a solution but didn't find one?"
- "How could you better cope with the worst that could occur in the event you are unable to cough up a solution?"
- "How might you be lost without the blind alleys that come from not finding a solution? In other words, what advantages might you find from your efforts in futility?"
- "When was the last time that you found out what 'had to be' never did turn up?"

122. "What is going to become of me?"
      A burning desire to be privy to what the future will bring burdens present happiness possibilities. Fortunately such knowledge doesn't exist and if it did it would rob life of anticipation and meaning due to having prior information as to what will eventually be all said and done. To belabor trying to find tomorrow's answers can be prevented by these recommendations and persuasions:

- "I would suggest that you first come to grips with the worst that could occur and then the rest of your concerns wouldn't exactly be chicken soup, but perhaps they would be less alarming."
- "What will be, will be, but I'm afraid you will be required to stick around in order to find out."
- "Would you enjoy the game as much if you knew the final tally ahead of time?"
- "Of what influence do you see yourself in determining the final score?"
- "In large part the answer to that question will likely be more determined by your own work habits."
- "In all probability you are going to live and you are going to die—your philosophy of effort in the interval will likely determine that status."

- "In whatever you attempt you will have a genetic floor and a genetic ceiling—whether you turn up on the floor or ceiling of your goals will in large part be decided by whether you sustain your good intentions with the right working methods."
- "Whether or not you take the roads with the extra mile most likely will tell a lot of what will (be made to) become of you."

123. "What is wrong with me wanting just good things and not wanting any bad things to happen?"
     Clients sometimes make themselves defensive about wanting the finer things in life. They rightly set reasonable and realistic goals that they desire for themselves—and then wrongly demand they be obtained. This question provides an opportunity to teach the client the value of preferential motivation and the handicap of making oneself demandingly insistent. Using this question as a takeoff for distinguishing between sensible preference and nonsensical demand is seen in these explanations:

- "Don't apologize for only wanting pleasure and wanting to avoid pain—you would be emotionally worse off if you *didn't* want pleasurable experience or *wanted* painful occurrences."
- "Even if there were something wrong with wanting what you want, you wouldn't be required to let that stop you from seeking those goals."
- "Nothing that I know of."
- "Although it might be a mite unfair to the rest of us if you got all of the good and none of the bad, that would be our problem—now wouldn't it?"
- "Be glad you have a philosophy of wanting to avoid the negative and at the same time lap up the positive—just don't make yourself so insistent that be the case."
- "What you have here seems to be part of a philosophy of enlightened self-interest, which is to be encouraged provided you don't elevate your wants to the realm of sacred demands."
- "To operate on the "seeking pleasure, avoiding pain" principle is one of those things that motivates one to make an OK life better."

- "Having knowledge of what you want is a grand thing, provided you are prepared to cut yourself some slack in the event things don't fall into place as expected."

124.   "You're going to laugh when I tell you what I am here for."
    By implication this statement is a form of self-deprecation. Often clients are accustomed to not being taken seriously and conclude that they or their requests and position statements are not worthy of consideration. They end up apologizing for themselves for having goals and ambitions. Convincing clients to view their objectives as serious and worthwhile—whether or not others do—requires them to be taught how to get themselves past their deprecatory bents. Picking up on their original slap-in-their-own-face-type statement above and directing them toward a more nonapologetic, staunch stance can begin with some of these counters and inquiries:

- "And if I did?"
- "If I or anyone else would laugh about your problems how would that cause them to be any less important?"
- "What's more important, whether you take your problems seriously or whether others do?"
- "What would be a good way for you to interpret it if I, or anyone else for that matter, would laugh at you?"
- "Would it be catastrophic or the cat's meow if I did?"
- "What do you presume someone giving your problems the limp and laughing hand tells you about you?"
- "Are you willing to risk being laughed at, scorned if not ridiculed, as a possible entry fee for putting your concerns out on the table?"
- "If you are laughed at for being openly honest about something that is important for you, what might that tell you about the person doing the laughing?"
- "What is the absolutely most horrifying thing that could happen when you are laughed at?"

125.   "Don't you think it's about time that I did something right?"

Clients' exaggerations and direct or implied self-put-downs are to be identified and replaced by more accurate cognitions. The faulty notion that a long period of time has elapsed since something has been done right by the client promotes hopelessness, listlessness, and inertia. Such a faulty inference stretches out the problem longer than it actually is. It also makes convenient a harsher negative rating of oneself for the supposed lengthy trail of errors. The wind of self-acceptance can be put back into the client's sails by challenging the dysfunctional conclusion of this question. This may be met with some resistance from the client in that truth is often a convenience item. If the client can convince himself that it has been near infinity since he did something right, he can more easily justify presently resting in this flawed pattern, rather than thinking in terms of rolling up his sleeves and trying again. Nevertheless, it is the therapist's responsibility to attempt to raise the consciousness of the client regarding his exaggeration of his mistake-ridden pattern. This can be accomplished through use of the following questions and counters:

- "How long a time are we talking about?"
- "Before I answer that question I'd like to know what you want to do right and how you plan to do so."
- "What have you been doing wrong that has prevented yourself from doing right more often?"
- "Why do you think it might be convenient for you to imply that it has been a month of Sundays since you have done something right?"
- "What do you think your string of wrongdoings tells you about you?"
- "How does a person survive with a lengthy history of not doing anything right?"
- "Anytime is the time to do something right."
- "Better late than never—but does the never really apply here?"

126. "Why am I this way?"
      There are realities to the human condition that won't go away. Perhaps the main ever-present characteristic is humans' remarkable natural fallibility. As a consequence of this lingering trait there are virtually no special reasons for personality development. Humans simply are born with inclinations, preferences, and tendencies, though with hard work these innate inclinations do not have to be made binding. The search for unique reasons is often made to go on, perhaps because of magic thinking that assumes if the whys and wherefores of personality formation are identified, somehow such insight by itself can result in change. The wishful thinking behind this question presumes that knowledge is the same as action, that knowing something about how something began will automatically control or change it. This paralysis of the analysis inquiry can be responded to by these rational promptings and rebuttals:

- "What leads you to believe that a special reason exists?"
- "Because you're a card-carrying member of the human race."
- "Would such knowledge, if available, cause action?"
- "Do you think it would be more advisable to do less figuring and stewing and more doing?"
- "What do you think would pose more difficulty, finding an answer to this question or finding a needle in a haystack?"
- "Is this a question whose answer one can be sure of?"
- "Do all haystacks have needles in them and what leads you to believe that this one does?"

127. "How can I feel important?"
      Many of the problems in the world are caused by people who think that they need to feel important. They then frantically try to fill in their bottomless-pit-of-recognition craving. A first step in therapeutically responding to this question would be to distinguish whether the client is wanting to be considered by herself as being important due to her existence and/or for her contributions to her social group or whether she indeed is escalating her de-

sire for importance into a demand for same. The following persuasions can be directed toward those in the latter, more frequently evidenced category in an effort to moderate the cravings and pangs of their recognition and admiration seeking:

- "By letting yourself to be so rather than proving yourself to be so."
- "By allowing rather than forcing yourself to feel so."
- "Simply by your own permission."
- "By willing it to yourself–for no extra charge."
- "By appreciating more fully the value you have to yourself and your ability to be an enjoying person."
- "By first disputing any ideas that insist that 'I must' feel important."
- "Do you simply want to feel important or do you more demandingly view it as a dire necessity?"

128. "How can I improve my self-confidence?"
   This frequent inquiry implies a nagging fear of failure. Unless it is discussed within a framework of failure as shattering being a misperception, the root problem will go unnoticed. "Improving my self-confidence" is a rather nebulous goal; getting after the fear of failure that it reflects has a clearer, substantive ring to it. If the client can be directly taught not to overreact to or personalize failure, the lack of self-confidence and failure as bigger-than-life problems can be tended to at the same time. Therapeutic responses that can serve as a mechanism for doing just that include:

- "Don't you really mean that you're dreadfully afraid of failure?"
- "What would your 'self-confidence' be like if you learned to intimidate yourself less by the possibility of failure?"
- "Do you think that learning how to more fully accept yourself would be a good starter?"
- "By welcoming rather than abhorring failure."

- "By continuing to try like hell to follow your pursuits, but not put yourself down when you flounder in the achievement of them."
- "By attaching more importance to what you think about yourself and your interests, and lesser value to what others conclude."
- "By coming to grips with the worst that could happen when you try something and not defining such worst-of-the-worst negative outcomes as being catastrophic or self-deprecating."
- "By leaving self-evaluation out of the self-confidence equation."
- "By strongly concluding that success would be nice, if not great—but not necessary."

129. "How can I like myself when I look in the mirror?"
     People who like or love themselves have few rivals. This "mirror, mirror, on the wall, how can I at least consider myself to be as fair, if not fairer than them all" question connotes the idea that special reasons are required to appreciate one's presence in the world. Teaching clients to identify and judge their traits, behaviors, and performances without judging themselves is a key to minimizing emotional disturbance. Observing oneself and how well one's own standards are followed is an important matter, but to define self, including how well one likes oneself, by self-observations is an anti-mental health endeavor on two fronts: (a) It promotes self-indulgence, me, me, me absorption in ego where the primary mission becomes proving alleged worth to self and social group; (b) It creates depression, guilt, and anxiety, the first two feeling states stemming from putting oneself down for faltering and the third one from anticipating putting yourself down in the event of failure. Far better is it to encourage clients to rip up their personal-accounting, esteem-building system so that they can zero in on unconditional self-acceptance. This can be done with these responses:

- "What do you think the idea 'Those who like themselves are likely to have few rivals' means?"

- "What do you think it would take to 'like yourself'?"
- "In finding special reasons to 'like yourself' do you think there is any danger of becoming a bottomless pit?"
- "What is your impression of those people you have known who 'like themselves'?"
- "You can like what you see by abiding by your standards of self-presentation, but give some consideration to leaving the liking-yourself ego out of it."
- "Try to differ between enjoying, being, accepting yourself, and liking yourself–which of these has more of an emotional relief flavor to it?"

130. "What if others find out?"
     Shame is an emotional problem in itself and it also serves to extend existing problems. If a person does the wrong thing and puts himself down for negative acts he will feel guilt; if he worries about others finding out about his wrongdoing, or if his errors do become public knowledge and he damns himself about others' disapproving views of traits or actions, he will give himself a bad case of shame. Desacredizing the importance of public scrutiny of mistakes is a strong counter against shame and can be implemented by such alternative thinking as:

- "If others judgmentally get wind of your mistakes, does that make them any more significant than before they knew of them?"
- "Short of becoming a hermit, what could you do to cope with others discovering that you are a fallible human being?"
- "Then they would."
- "Let's say they thought less of you, if not hated you, for your blunders. Would you have to hate yourself?"
- "What do you think are some ways to more helpfully and emotionally healthfully override public disclosure of your flaws?"
- "Could you not live with yourself, if not still enjoy yourself, in spite of public awareness of your failings?"

- "One choice would be to challenge yourself to not become depressed even in the throes of other disclosure."

131. "What if I fall flat on my face?"

    Because humans tend to think in extremes, they waste considerable time worrying about "bombing out" or "totally failing." Such catastrophic concerns are more likely to bring on this proverbial fear due to their anxiety-producing fallout. Meeting the total-extinction implications of this question head-on can be done with these directives:

- "Then you would have a flattened face."
- "Your question implies that 'flatly' failing would mean 'all,' 'one hundred percent,' or 'more than bad' of an experience. Might you be exaggerating a bit here?"
- "Then we would have something in common."
- "Your personality well-roundedness may be increased by leaps and bounds."
- "As the philosopher Nietzsche said, 'That which does not kill me, makes me stronger.' How will 'falling flat' on your face give you the opportunity to strengthen yourself?"
- "Others could grow to like you more, as you model 'perfect' human fallibility."
- "You could beat others to the punch by laughing at yourself before they do."
- "You could look for the best in the worst and let it be a lesson to be learned now and used in the future."

132. "After all these years of trying I should at least have made some progress, if not succeeded by now."

    Beneath this tenor of frustration lies a voiced demand for fairness, deservingness, justice, and reciprocation. However, paybacks, though nice, do not occur in orderly cycles. Showing the client the value of expecting less return on effort invested can help pave the way for fuller emotional well-being. Such suggested acceptance can be viewed through the following therapeutic comebacks:

- "Is there really a universal formula that designates success as accompanying each increment of effort?"
- "Success comes when it gets here and not a moment before—regardless of your time and energy devotions."
- "What do you think Tom Edison said to himself after 600 attempts, when he still had not invented electricity?"
- "What does the notion mean that apparently you should not have succeeded or even made progress yet, because you haven't?"
- "It sounds like you're protesting against the fact that you haven't succeeded or made progress; if so, who or what are you protesting to?"
- "What kind of feelings follow the 'should'?"
- "What would be a better way to look at your lack of progress?"
- "Do you view this as a grim reality or *too* grim a one?"
- "What are some things that you have learned from falling short of the mark for so long that you may not have learned had you succeeded earlier in the game?"

133. "I'm out of touch with my feelings. How can I tell what they are?"
   One of the myths of problem solving is that clients are "out of touch with their feelings." My observation is that a large majority of clients are very much in touch with their feelings—that they are quite aware when they feel anger, guilt, fear, depression. What they are out of touch with is a method of better controlling what they well know exists. Yet, for the minority who plead ignorance to their feelings, perhaps the best way to help them come out of the dark is to identify, in collaboration with them, their beliefs that preceded and largely caused their feelings. These are ordinarily ideas that reflect demandingness, exaggeration, and blame, e.g., "I/you/the world must do well by me and it is horrible when this does not occur; damn me/others/the world when I am treated by self/others/life with lapses in perfectionistic competence, kindness, and consideration." The following comments

and suggestions respond to this plea for feeling identification:

- "Look for the strength and the length of what you feel; the stronger and longer it is, the harsher its content."
- "The ultimate tip-off would be your thoughts about your circumstances and others in it. Let's try to make a thought-feeling connection about a feeling in question."
- "Do you mean you don't know how to control them?"
- "Don't jump to conclusions; for instance if you're sad don't presume you're depressed; or if you feel annoyed don't assume anger."
- "Learn the anatomy of your common unwanted emotions; start this by learning to identify in your beliefs the demands, exaggerations, and self- and other downings that set them off."
- "Don't pretend to not know what you do know. If you do feel anger, fear, and other emotions don't be ashamed to admit it."

134. "It took me a long time to get (myself) this way, so it's going to take a long time for me to change."
      This presumptuous, self-fulfilling promise is often a rationalization for taking one's sweet-natured time about revising one's thoughts, feelings, and behaviors. It discourages its holder from exerting the energy required to accelerate personal change. Immediate comfort is experienced from this lax, lulling idea. Although it is often true that one has more time than money, this is no excuse to complacently move as slowly as molasses in January in tackling problems. Getting across to clients that although it could take a chunk of time to change, does not mean that it will, can be done with these notations:

- "What goes up does not necessarily come down as slowly as it went up."
- "Untying yourself is quicker than tying yourself up."
- "Can you think of examples from your own life or from others where change was made to occur quickly—even though the problem had a lengthy existence?"

- "Problems can be made to linger or they can be made not to linger–the choice is for the most part yours."
- "The person who says the same problem is going to take a long time to solve and the person who says it is going to take a short time to undo–are often *both* right."
- "Do you think there could be any exceptions to this rule?"
- "How can you see to it that this one-size formula doesn't fit all?"
- "Are not humans capable of more rapid-fire, quick change?"
- "What do you say we try to break tradition by making the length of the solution shorter than the length of the problem?"

135. "How can I feel more comfortable while changing my-self?"
      This question is often turned into an insistence, e.g., "I want to feel more comfortable so therefore I must." A few things in life come easy, like trouble and hassle. However, when it comes to making personal changes that are good for us to make there is practically always an entry fee of discomfort. In part this is simply the human tendency to fear change with an unknown outcome. Avoiding the comfort trap with clients can be accomplished with these spoken realities:

- "How comfortable is comfortable enough for you?"
- "Is comfort essential or just desirable?"
- "You're not going to turn yourself into a comfort junkie now, are you?"
- "Keep in mind that most things in life worth accomplishing have a feeling of discomfort along with them; this is because of the force and effort ordinarily required to arrive at your desired destination."
- "By uncomfortably meeting the requirements of making changes for the better and, in doing so, helping yourself to feel more comfortable in the *long* run."
- "By accepting present pain for future gain."
- "By doing the right thing today, realizing that you will feel better tomorrow."

- "By tallying up the advantages of your changes and vividly calling them to mind a dozen or two times per day."

136. "Who is to blame for all of this?"
     To err is human; to blame is even more human. The proclaimed necessity of fixing blame, namely on someone other than yours truly, is related to the belief that someone must be blamed—and better you than me! When the advisability of blaming someone is dimmed the problem-solving light is more likely to go on. By trying not to fix blame, cooperation between participants is begun through fighting the problem instead of fighting each other. Moving away from this common fingerpointing direction can be encouraged by these suggestive rational responses:

- "What would be better, to fix blame or to fix the problem?"
- "What do you think would become of the problem if you transferred the energy it takes to blame someone to the seeking of a solution?"
- "Which is a better investment, in blame or in correction?"
- "It's true that someone may be at fault for this predicament, but what would be accomplished by blaming whoever that might be?"
- "Is our goal to curse the darkness or to light candles?"
- "To err is human; to blame is even more human—yet inhumane."
- "What about all those happenings that occur for no special reason. How can we legitimately account for them—and would it be worth it?"
- "How will blaming change anything that has happened or create solutions to problems that could happen?"

137. "What would other people think?"
     Much of what is called anxiety is an overconcern for what others might think of us. Responding to this question in a comprehensive way can help dissolve the malady of disapproval anxiety. Freeing clients to be themselves with minimal concern for others' estimations of

their efforts is no small favor. Questions and comments that contribute to encouraging inner- rather than other-directedness include:

- "What cosmic significance do you foresee that would have for you?"
- "In that people are different, probably different from you, some would likely think the worst, others the best—after all—one man's meat is another man's poison."
- "Are you implying that you want to please all of the people all of the time? If you are—lots of luck!"
- "What is the very worst others could think about this matter—and how could you not let it get under your skin?"
- "What are some examples of others' critical reviews of you and your performances, and how did you manage to survive it so far?"
- "Many humans tend to believe the worst in others rather than in themselves, so what would be your rough guess?"
- "How can you use this negativity, not to work wonders for your mental health, but to improve upon it?"

138. "There must be better choices than this!"
    Sometimes the best solution to a problem is to accept that there may not be a smorgasbord of possibilities in regard to righting the situation. This demand, unless rationally addressed, contributes to self-pity and giving up. The therapist can persuade the clients to give themselves a fighting chance with the choices they have rather than bemoaning alternatives they don't have, by using these countering messages:

- "Oftentimes what you see is what you get by way of possibilities."
- "And if there isn't . . . ?"
- "Because your possibilities are limited doesn't necessarily mean that it's not possible to come out ahead."
- "Where is it carved in granite that there must be?"
- "Because you lack solution possibilities doesn't mean you're doomed; it simply means that you will be required to use the

options you have and hopefully not scream about those that you don't have."
- "Often quality of choices is much more important than quantity."
- "Persist with the choices you have; don't resist using them. Persist—don't resist."
- "Frequently one doesn't know what might be better until one tries what is in hand."
- "Try the alternatives you have and then continue with newer choices that might occur to you from what you learned as a result of your efforts."

139. "I have to do *my* best, right?"
      Clients communicate their perfectionism in varying ways. As a consequence of their exactness they put much strain on daily living. One brand of perfectionism that often goes unnoticed is the notion of giving one's highest performance possible, meaning 100 percent maximum effort. This view does not allow for human error or letdown and consequently results in fear of failing. This causes eventual self-blame when one inevitably fails to produce and/or achieve at this perfectionistic level. More flexible, permissive conclusions that lead to emotional slack and consequently greater enjoyment of and achievement in the task at hand can be seen in these well-thought-out rejoinders:

- "Try to do well without thinking that you have to try to accomplish perfectly well."
- "Scientifically, nothing as far as can be seen is 100 percent, including your *better* efforts."
- "Realistically, you don't *have to* do anything but you may *want to* put out a lot of good effort."
- "If you were able to give it your best you might not have much energy for the next go-around."
- "Wrong! Gather your resources and try to apply them within the limitations of your skills in doing so."

- "If you think that it is only right that you must do 'your best,' what is your guess as to how you will feel when you sooner, rather than later, don't hit the bull's-eye of doing so?"

140. "I have to prove it to myself and to others."
    This insistence hints at ego problems that unless exposed will go underground and undermine emotional well-being. Clients often do the right things, e.g., succeed, for the wrong reasons, e.g., for self- and/or other proving motivations rather than simply for serving one's self-interest. The following comments and inquiries combat self- and other esteem-building motivations and replace them with incentives that are more self-advantageous while leaving ego and disapproval anxieties on the doorstep:

- "How is this self- and other proving matter so essential for you?"
- "And if you don't, what in your view will that tell you about you?"
- "Would there be any advantages of being yourself without strenuously trying to prove yourself?"
- "With this declaration in hand do you sleep any better, worse, or about the same?"
- "Are you trying to prove 'it' to yourself or trying to more literally prove yourself?"
- "What advantages do you see for yourself in winning such a proving shootout?"
- "Would such 'provingness' end there or might such self- and other demonstrations be made to go on indefinitely?"
- "Where have such white-knuckled efforts of ego and other mania got you in the past?"
- "What are some characteristics that you have noticed in others who put themselves through the rigor of proving something to self and to others?"

141. "How come *nobody* else has this kind of problem?"
    Normalization or the idea that eleven out of ten people have emotional and behavioral problems is supportive in

that it provides the client with the comfort of knowing that they are not alone by way of human unhappiness. Such liberal teachings pave the way for constructive learnings regarding the problem(s) at hand. Suggesting that the client not exaggerate the isolation of his/her problem can be done with these reality counters:

- "How broadly have you surveyed this hypothesis?"
- "If 'nobody' has this problem, what are some problems that come close to it?"
- "It's hard to imagine you as the only person in this big world who has this strain of genetic deficiency."
- "How many kinds of problems do you think there are?"
- "When you use the word 'nobody' aren't you stretching it a bit in defining yourself as living in such a unique problem-entity territory?"
- "Why would you be so cursed and not any other?"
- "Let's give you the benefit of the huge doubt and agree that 'nobody' else has this God-forsaken problem. Of what significance is that when it comes to your solving it?"
- "All right, such uniqueness allows you the opportunity of making history by at least putting a dent in this problem that nobody apparently has ever had the misfortune of having. What do you think of them apples?"

142.   "He has no right to repeatedly make the same mistake." Clients often make it crystal clear that when it comes to accepting others' mistakes there are definite limits on their tolerance and forgiveness capacities. Once forgiven—maybe, but twice or more—for sure not. Sometimes a client's rulebook accepts another's wrongdoing—as long as such errors are not made to chronically reoccur. Unfortunately humans are well known, though not well accepted, for making the same mistake over and over again. This is seen in the grim reality that most of the traits we don't like in others, which we also possess, aren't made to change all that much! This is unlike a client who announced to me, "The next time I come to see you I won't have made the same mistake again—I'll make a

new one." The idea of accepting others *without* the condition that they not make a repeated error can be promoted with these declaratives:

- "How does this idea cushion you for the realities of the remarkably fallible human condition?"
- "Who says or where is it written that this statement bears a semblance to reality?"
- "Are there any others in the universe, besides yourself, who have an injunction filed against the repeat offender?"
- "If 'to err is human' wouldn't 'to repeatedly err' also be so?"
- "What percentage of humans would you say (frequently) violate this doctrine of nonrepetitive error as the route one must go?"
- "Where do human limitations and free will infiltrate into your equation?"

143. "Don't you agree with me that there are some things who people should never do?"
      Practically everyone has a sacred cow that defies facts of the human condition as they relate to free will and human limitations. As difficult as it is to dislodge sacred ideals it is often worth it from a mental health standpoint. If a person does something, then they did it; there are no shoulds about it. There are many acts that are undesirable because they are against personal and/or societal best interests. Such acts would be well to be discouraged. Making this distinction between the many negative behaviors that are to be discouraged via enforcement of negative consequences and those same conducts that are likely to continue to occur (though hopefully less often due to enforcement of the hell to pay following them) can be a significant factor in preventing emotional wear and tear. Whether another's conduct is 360 degrees plus some light-years apart from one's treasured values is beside the point. Responses that point to the use of logic and reason in minimizing damnation of and overreaction to another's deplorable behaviors include:

- "To quote George Bernard Shaw: 'The only golden rule is that there is no golden rule.'"
- "There are many behaviors not recommended for human consumption, but that doesn't mean that they can't be consumed."
- "By demanding that others not balk at your exalted sacred cows you put yourself at risk of becoming the very enemy that you speak of."
- "I agree with human preference, but not with human demand."
- "I think that the best we can do is to steer people into hardly ever committing certain heinous acts, but 'never' is a long time."
- "How is it possible to get everyone to always think alike on the advisability of whether to engage in a given behavior or not?"
- "For better or for worse people apparently are going to do what they are going to do regardless of any universal laws that we may try to establish."
- "If it's harshly cold outside, why shouldn't it be, if it is?"

144.   "Does therapy work?"
Clients naturally want something advantageous from their therapy–they want it to work for them. From the onset it would be better to communicate to them that time and elbow grease from them will most likely determine outcome, that their active participation in the activity is likely to be required in order to forge a successful outcome. The stouthearted message that clients will be expected to work for and with their therapy so as to build a well-rounded rather than a one-sided therapeutic alliance is seen in these countering expectations:

- "Hopefully you will form a united front with your therapy so as to take on a double-barreled approach to helping yourself."
- "Get on the side of your therapy and work for and with it."
- "Ask not what your therapy can do for you, ask what you can do for your therapy."
- "Nothing works but working, including with and for your therapy."
- "Learning is not a spectator sport, nor is therapy."

- "Active participation rather than passive bystanding prompts results."

145. "How can I ever amount to anything?"
    The search for the eternal fountain of worth continues with this question regarding self-estimation. The sooner clients learn that what they do is not the same as who they are, the sooner they will be able to avoid self-measurement trappings. Personal insecurity is revealed in trying to combine a tally that will once and for all substantiate a high amount of worth. Most people secretly or not so secretly harbor thoughts of inferiority and self-deprecation that they desperately try to perfume by itemizing their strengths and advantages and then judge themselves by them. The problem with this question is that there is no legitimate or provable answer to it. Rational inquiries that try to relinquish this "horse with no name" type question include:

- "What 'amount' are you looking for?"
- "Do you see yourself as measurable?"
- "What do you mean by 'amount'?"
- "What is the ratio of your measuring cup? How much of this or that is equal to the amount you're worth because of such ingredients and attributes?"
- "Who is the judge and jury in this measuring bee; who has the final say-so in who cuts muster, who doesn't, and by how much?"
- "It sounds like you want to use your capabilities as a measuring rod to prove what amount you're worth."
- "Technically, no human can amount to anything in that humans are not rateable, but that doesn't mean that you can't learn to gain more advantages and have more of a ball in life."
- "I think it's possible to itemize the amount of your advantages and the amount of fun you have in life but whatever those amounts might be doesn't prove that you have 'amounted' to anything–it simply means that you have accumulated some good things (and hopefully in good amount)."

146. "Why can't I ever win at anything?"

Too bad that four-leaf clovers don't bring good luck. If they did, those who think that they are down on their luck could go out in their backyard and pick one while expecting to win the next lottery or at whatever else their heart desires. Most people not only believe in luck but also demand their fair share of it. They beef when they consistently don't win, which is bound to often happen simply because there will likely be many others competing for the same advantages. Helping clients to accept that there is only so much room in the inn for the victors encourages them to rely more on themselves and less on chance. Confrontive ideas that can assist in accepting this statistical disadvantage, yet trying to do something about it, include:

- "What have you learned by losing that has led to eventually winning?"
- "Is the word 'ever' more than a slight exaggeration?"
- "Have there ever been times you have lost and were glad that you did?"
- "You don't win as often as you would like simply because there are so many others vying for the same thing."
- "Do you see your losing plight as being statistically different from that of the masses?"
- "When is the last time you came close to winning and what were you doing right that had you extended it further, might have increased your chances of going all the way?"
- "When you're down on your 'luck,' as you call it, do you get down on yourself or do other things that detract from future success possibilities?"

147. "But I've been this way all my life."

To teach an older or young client new tricks usually is met with some resistance. A love affair with the status quo and the immediate comfort it produces is expressed through this resistive question. Getting clients past the irrational idea that because something has been made to occur up until now, it is mandated to continue to be made to occur, can be done with these options of expression:

- "Is it a must that history be made to continue to be repeated?"
- "If you ate eggshells all your life would you be required to continue to bite away on them?"
- "Have there been patterns of thought, emotion, and/or behavior that you have managed to do a turnaround on?"
- "How much time of your life do you think that you have left to modify this pattern—if you would choose to?"
- "Do your choices stop with this apparent fact of your life?"
- "Give an example of someone you know who has reversed direction in his/her life and what would you guess would be some of his/her secrets that allowed this to happen?"
- "So are you planning on waiting for the next life before you change?"
- "All right, but how long would you consider it to be long enough and enough is enough?"

148. "I'm afraid that if I stop trying to be perfect, I'll just give up."

   While it is true that the human tendency is to go from one extreme to the other, such inclinations are not required to be made binding. Because you accept your non-Godlike capabilities and yourself with them does not mean that you must now go from perfectionism and the pursuit of unhappiness to slovenliness and the pursuit of unhappiness. Overdoing and underdoing are both equally destructive in that they arrive from a stance of faulty perceptions as to what the situation calls for. Throwing in the towel because you think you would be a louse if you continued to try and fail, and perfectionistically driving yourself out of fear of failure is the same ego problem with a different brand name. This question containing problems of the extreme can be badgered with these alternative responses:

- "In any two extremes is not the truth often someplace in between?"
- "Moderation seems to be against your religion."

- "Between the east and the west are there not many places?"
- "What is it that you honestly are afraid of?"
- "Each of these similar fear-of-failure hearses with different license plates (perfectionism and laziness) can be the death of you–if you let them."
- "Put away the halos, wings, and pitchforks that represent self-judgments, and see what happens."
- "If you gave up the impossible dream of being perfect, what would prevent you from continuing to press forward in hopes of goal achievement?"
- "How does the idea of your putting more emphasis on getting yourself vitally absorbed in doing well, minus the perfectly part, strike you?"

149. "I'm afraid that if I stop myself from feeling highly upset, I won't have any feelings at all."
    A common irrational idea of what constitutes rational is that to be so is to be without feelings. However, giving up emotional disturbance is a far cry from giving up feelings. It is important to educate clients on the distinction between feeling replacement and feeling abandonment. The latter is more befitting for a robot than a human. Replacing anger with displeasure, fear with apprehension and concern, guilt with regret, and depression with sorrow can be done so that the client is made aware of how he can create appropriate feelings (those that are in his best interests) rather than inappropriate feelings (those that are against his best interests). Squelching or eliminating feelings is not part of the rational game plan. Thoughtful responses that correct the client misnomer of "no feelings" include:

- "In any two extremes, the truth lies someplace in the middle ground."
- "This sounds like a theory more fit for a robot than a human."
- "What do you think of the idea of exploring the difference between feelings that are in your best interests and those that are against your best interests–but forsake the forever-stone-face notion."

- "There is a difference between thinking differently and feeling differently and thinking differently and having no feelings at all."
- "Before you got yourself to the point of being highly upset you made yourself feel less frustrated along the way. What can you do to reverse your feelings to a less harsh state?"
- "Like a lot of things, feelings are not all or nothing; there are also shades of grey to consider."
- "Dissolving anger, fear, guilt, and depression is light-years away from dissolving feelings."
- "If you can stop yourself from feeling highly upset as you imply, it is likely that you can stop yourself from abandoning feelings in total."

150. "If I give up on this matter I might give up on everything."
     This position is yet another example of extremism and all-or-nothing thinking that typifies the human condition. Teaching clients to lessen overgeneralized thinking tendencies is important as it allows them to more accurately see what they are up against, better consider alternatives, and aspire to hope. Questions and comments that can prevent clients from playing leap-frog thinking are:

- "What is to stop you from not duplicating the giving-up mentality?"
- "Does one incidence really constitute a pattern?"
- "Can a distinction be made between a slip and a continuous pattern?"
- "You might if you chose to, but must you choose to?"
- "Watch your rubber-band thinking where you stretch possibilities into inevitabilities."

151. "Isn't it about time for others to start cooperating with me?"
     Insistences upon cooperation as the action component of agreement explains much relationship upheaval. To get any two (to say nothing about more) people to cooperatively support one another is unusual. Furthermore, there

is no timetable for such agreement and when an attempt is made to establish one forcefully, the sparks really fly. Getting clients to step back from such an ultimatum makes for a less conflictual, more harmonious engagement. This dictatorial question can be tamed down by these buffering rebuttals:

- "Your time is not necessarily their time."
- "What might be some reasons others are not yet ready, willing, and able to cooperate with you?"
- "And if they don't . . . ?"
- "What standardized measuring rod are you going by?"
- "If it is, apparently they don't know it."
- "How can you make do until they find out what you seem to know?"
- "How long would you intend to wait for them to do so before you give some consideration to the possibility that the time may never come?"
- "Are you reasonably sure that they agree with you enough to be capable of cooperating with you–if not, you may be putting the cart before the horse."

152. "What do I do when I can't count on anybody?"
   Self-reliance in the face of others' unreliability is especially important in that others are much more often than not for their values and projects and therefore cannot be looked to for any degree of consistent assistance in tracking your goals. This question, which by implication borders on self-pity en route to sulking, can be sprightly responded to by way of these counters:

- "Option number one: look to little bitty old you."
- "One of the things that you can practically always do is count on yourself."
- "It depends on what your goals are–if independence, then forge ahead by yourself; if dependence, then wait for someone to do your work for you."
- "Apparently if your goals are to be reached it's going to be up to you."

- "What do you think of the idea of counting on yourself and letting it go at that?"
- "Search for the advantages of others' staying out of your way by their not trying to help."
- "Don't punt; plow ahead instead."
- "Do what you can rather than stew about what others won't do."
- "Count on yourself rather than count yourself out."
- "Due to others' refusals reaching epidemic proportions you will be required to work extra hard to get decent results, but remember—nothing works but working."

153. "Why can't I just once get their approval?"
   A crumb or two for a starving person isn't much. Neither does a tad of approval do much for emotional sustenance. The client's dire need for approval is embedded in this question and unless uprooted and challenged will raise havoc with one's emotions. A dab of approval today may temporarily pacify your emotions but it will not make for more permanent emotional rustproofing. Rebuttals that will uncover the approval requirements underlying this longing inquiry are:

- "What price are you willing to pay to get it?"
- "And how will that sustain you over time?"
- "Are you sure that once would be enough?"
- "Because your values are so much at odds with one another."
- "You make it sound so essential; is it?"
- "A taste may lead to want for more if not to a bottomless pit. How might that be so?"
- "Rather than seek a crumb or two, wouldn't it be better to learn how to bake your own bread?"
- "Does your emotional life depend upon this elusive happening?"

154. "Why can't you do any more for me?"
   Instant and total relief is what clients often expect. When their magical hopes are dashed they complain. Part of therapy is leveling with clients what to realistically ex-

pect of you and the therapy you offer. By setting down-to-earth boundaries on the potential benefits of the helping endeavor, pie-in-the-sky illusions can be avoided. Persuasions that comply with honest expectations while suggesting a decent respect for human limitations, including your own ability to help, are:

- "Perhaps my well has run dry."
- "Believe me, I'm trying."
- "What are some advantages of my not being able to go full circle for you?"
- "Because I'm limited, *not* limitless."
- "What might you be looking for that has not been found already?"
- "First do a little more for yourself and see if I can't trigger further suggestions after that."
- "Because though I'm ready and willing, I may not be able to."
- "How much more do you want me to do and is there a limit to what that might be?"

155. "Why can't I just forget about the past?"
Wanting to put the handicaps of the past behind is a wise ambition; attempting to block out these adversities by not remembering them goes against natural human recall. Rephrasing the goal to forget the past so that the client continues to retrieve memories but to think about them in a more tolerant, accepting way would be a more possible goal to consciously process through the past. Comments and questions that follow this more realistic view of human consciousness about the past are:

- "Forgetting the past might also include forgetting what you learned from it."
- "Do you want to forget about the past or remember it in a different way?"
- "Forgetting the past prevents an 'all things considered' understanding of yourself."
- "Experiences don't die, though they can be interpreted differently."

- "Because some of your present conclusions were inspired by your past experiences."
- "To deny what existed is not an easy thing."
- "Sometimes it's because the person is demanding that the past be different than it was."
- "To force forgetfulness is to assure remembrance."
- "There are some things in life that you can't force yourself to do, only allow yourself to, such as remembering to forget to remember!"
- "Maybe you're trying too hard."

156. "How come I had to be raised in such a crummy family?"

    Having parents who are human yet undisturbed in any way would be nothing short of a minor miracle. This question hopes against hope that such an extraordinary event occur. Imperfect, 'disturbed" families in an imperfect world are the norm. Accepting, if not finding advantages to, this ongoing reality is the therapeutic task. Inquiries and pointed comments that can aid in doing that include:

- "Because your parents and their offspring had such crummy gene pools."
- "Due to the multiple hazards of the human condition."
- "You were dealt a bad hand. Now how can you play it well?"
- "Because you don't have the luck of the Irish."
- "What makes you think that there is a special reason that is answerable to you?"
- "From a practical, get-a-move-on-with-your-life standpoint, what difference does it make?"
- "Because it provides you with the luxury of being able to use others' close-at-hand problems to work against your own."

157. "It seems to come so easy for other people, why doesn't it for me?"

    People are not born equal; some have more skills, resources, and advantages than others due to their genetic and social strata endowments. For some, abilities that secure advantages—e.g., reading, writing, arithmetic, test taking—come easy; for others, nothing comes easy but trouble. A central helping idea to communicate to clients is that due to skill deficiencies in many areas, they are going to be required to work, work, and work some more in a persistent effort to get what they want out of the one life they will ever have. The following questions and statements are designed to assist clients in accepting this shoulder-to-the-wheel, nose-to-the-grindstone philosophy:

- "Because though you were born free, you weren't born equal."
- "What seems effortless in others may require much effort for you to get to that point of accomplishment."
- "Different people, different skill levels."
- "Because you may have a handicap that they apparently don't."
- "Doing something naturally or easily practically always follows mastery of skills; perhaps you haven't yet mastered the required skills."
- "If you ask these folks how long they have been practicing what do you think most would tell you?"

158.   "Why were my parents so against me?"
       More than 99 percent of parents are for their children's best interests rather than against them. Yet, many children and, to a lesser degree, adult children, see it otherwise. They insist that their parents had nothing else better to do than to discriminate against them. They miss their parents' good intentions and instead personalize their often frantic, poor methods. Inviting adult children in particular to stop crowing about the fact that they were not the one child in the universe who had sane parents can be done with these alternative ways of commenting upon this nagging question:

- "They weren't so dumb." (Done humorously by the counselor.)
- "Who do you think takes you more seriously—your parents or yourself?"

- "Could it be that their harsh correction was more a vote of confidence because they believed you could do better, rather than because they hated you?"
- "Did they more damn your behaviors or did they damn you along with your cruddy acts?"
- "What do you think of the idea that if your parents were against you they simply wouldn't have bothered to try to light a fire under you?"
- "Let's just say that they really did have nothing else better to do than to be against you. How could you not let that stop you from being for yourself?"
- "In some ways it was good that they criticized and yelled at you as this gave them an avenue, perhaps the best one they knew of, for expressing their love and concern for you."
- "Perhaps when they gave you the corrective raspberries it was their way of telling you that there were conditions attached to your relationship with them. Can you imagine anything so awesome—a relationship with conditions attached to it?"

159. "Why can't I just snap out of it?"
   Humans are not like switches or hot and cold running water. Since they are not able to change their feelings instantaneously, this results in smoother problem solving. Accepting this reality buys patience, and patience produces more prudent problem-solving results. Conveying to clients that they may well be capable of coming out of their problems, though not snapping out of them, can be done via these rejoinders:

- "Because emotions don't run in the twinkling of an eye."
- "Because overcoming problems ordinarily takes practice, and practice takes time."
- "Look for changes in degree at first, not kind—a lesser degree of frequency of your problematic expression; a lightened intensity of your upset; and a shortened length of time before you dissolve your disturbance."
- "Because in life generally, and in emotional self-control specifically, life is not a snap, a crackle, or a pop."

- "Because you're running on 'human,' with-feelings time rather than on robot, without-feelings time."
- "It takes some time to forget, or better yet, to remember differently life's occurrences and also to forgive those who were involved in them."
- "We're not talking hot and cold running water here."

160. "Whatever possessed me to do that?"

Perhaps the most basic postulate underlying Cognitive-Behavior Therapy (CBT) generally, and Rational Emotive Behavior Therapy (REBT) specifically, is that someone or something outside of you doesn't magically wiggle into your head and give you a thought or mysteriously squirm into your gut and provide you with a feeling; nobody or nothing possesses you—you possess yourself. Getting this mythical "possessed" abracadabra, hocus-pocus monkey off your back best precede cognitive-behavior problem solving. Communicating to clients that they create and possess their own constructs and are not possessed by eerie, transpersonal phenomena helps set the groundwork for responsible problem solving. Questions and explanations that can prompt such groundbreaking ventures are:

- "The biggest obstacle to your own enlightenment is . . . you."
- "Because only you can possess yourself, only you have the resources to undo such an entanglement."
- "Unless you believe in demons, I'm not sure."
- "Your own overreactions, demands, and blamings—to name a few possibilities."
- "What are the clues that lead you to believe that there is a 'whatever' involved here?"
- "Who do you think ties and can untie your emotional straitjacket?"
- "If there is such a force and you can locate it you could probably sue it for entrapment—and live off the interest."

161. "Isn't it so much easier not to try?"

Inertia can be made into a tempting matter but do not lead

clients into this lulling perspective. Do-nothing-ism has an unusual sense of appeal due to its immediate comfort halo. To back away from a project does provide immediate emotional relief that is associated with not calling on oneself to expend energy. All decisions have consequences attached to them; deciding to opt for up-front relief is no exception. Getting clients to convince themselves that the pleasure of the moment frequently leads to pain later on is a cornerstone of good problem solving. Rebuttals that can assist in planting such seeds of consequential thinking are:

- "Is it also so much easier to die than it is to live?"
- "Not trying guarantees failure; how can failing be easier?"
- "Are you talking about today or down the road?"
- "Why might it *not* be easy to take the easy way out?"
- "What do you think is better—wearing out or rusting out?"
- "Talk to those who have tried to make a living off of not trying and see if they think it's easier not to try—over the course of a lifetime, that is."
- "Which is more economical: Present gain for future pain or present pain for future gain; short-run gain for long-run sacrifice or short-run sacrifice for long-run gain?"
- "You lose strength, momentum, and effort by not trying; you gain them by trying—therefore it's easier to try."

162. "But I don't like being treated unfairly."

This complaint is a legitimate one in that unfairness frequently dominates the human condition. Because others often select against us and due to the random nature of the universe, unfairness prevails with high regularity. The therapeutic task is to first show clients that it is in their best interest to not like to be treated unfairly, for if they favored such unfairness they would be much worse off than they already are. Second, once they see the advantages of having a strong preference for fair treatment see that they make it a point not to escalate that preference into a demand by telling themselves "Because I prefer fair treatment from the world and the people in it—they absolutely must shine up to me with never-ending bias." Encouraging the preference and following up with a discouragement of the demand can be illustrated by these statements and comments:

- "Be glad you don't like being treated unfairly. If you liked having your face in the mud, you would have much worse problems than you already have."
- "So, perhaps you don't like a lot of things, but why must they not exist because of your dislike?"
- "Realize that you don't like something that often defines the human condition, and then decide how you would do well to cope with its often present existence."
- "What are some emotionally healthy ways you have seen others cope with unfair treatment?"
- "What do you have a bigger say-so in, doing away with unfairness or dealing with it better?"
- "Do you see yourself being different from the rest of us as far as bearing the brunt of unfair treatment and then not liking it?"
- "How does one realistically go about the business of garnering fairer treatment?"

163.   "How do I know that it isn't going to get any worse?"
The insistence that things not go from bad to worse will frequently bring on the dreaded worst. Two important life postulates to get across to clients are to accept that they can't know beyond a shadow of a doubt that matters of concern won't get further out of hand, and if they unfortunately would, they are capable of calling upon their resources of tolerance and acceptance to better roll with the adversarial punches. Responses that can help to accomplish these important mental health principles are:

- "What does one know for sure these days?"
- "You don't—so therefore . . . ."
- "You could wish upon a star, but that may be of dubious value."
- "Rather than trying to guess whether or not there is a silver lining or more storm clouds behind the original ones, it might

be better to attend to your concerns by readying yourself for the worst without preoccupying yourself with that challenge."
- "What do you think your chances are of catching up with tomorrow's answers today?"
- "Is this goal actually reachable?"
- "What good does it do to raise impossible questions if you can't connect them with outcome answers?"

164. "If I know better, why don't I do what is better?"
Knowing something and using it are often worlds apart. As William Shakespeare said, "The whole world well knows, but nobody knows well." It's not what you know in and about life that is more important, rather it is what you do with what you know that puts bread on the table. Insisting that the action component be part and parcel of problem solving is a central condition of helping others to help themselves. After all, what good are tools unless you actually use them? Teaching the knowledge-action connection, without which counseling will run amuck, can be done through a combination of understanding and forced action. Doing what is better can precede knowing why you haven't done so up until now. Granted, it is preferable to come from a background of understanding of how you block and sabotage your own best interests. However, such a self-attunement reservoir is not a prerequisite for personal change. A "doing gets it done" manner of attack on the problem will suffice. Instruct clients to start by getting started—preferably with fuller understanding of self in hand—but also without too much ado about self-analysis. This can be accomplished by these counters:

- "Perhaps because you have spent too much time trying to figure out the 'why don't I's' to the neglect of the 'what will I's.' "
- "Because you haven't made enough effort to make the knowledge-action connection."
- "Spend more time forging and less figuring—and see what you can make happen."

- "Perhaps because you have let your lethargy continue to rest to the neglect of putting your ideas to a test. Test, don't rest."
- "You have let yourself drift by following the line of least resistance, not seeing that it will likely turn out to be the line of most resistance."
- "Because you have chosen to be a spectator rather than a player."
- "Because you haven't made clear enough to yourself the long-range disadvantages of not doing what is better."
- "You dropped the ball because you gave yourself butter fingers and let yourself slip away from the action component of helping yourself."
- "Because you aren't allowing yourself to see that the pleasure of the avoidant moment often leads to pain later on."
- "Halting upon the brink of action by making a spoken decision seems easier because you save yourself the immediate blood, sweat, and tears that are the entry fees for making a doing decision."

CONCLUSION

There you have it, approximately 1,000 rational rebuttals and the rationales behind each for more efficiently fielding clients' curve balls while increasing your therapeutic batting average with them. They will not fit for all of your clients all of the time, but most are distinctive enough to be used on selective occasions. With so much psychological armament at your disposal to extend clinical conversation, smoke out resistance, confront self-defeating conclusions, and question conventional wisdom, how can you go wrong? Assertively, yet often with humorous goodwill, go to clients. Don't wait for them to come to you in your efforts to not take them as seriously as they practically always take themselves.

Long-lasting therapeutic benefits are most likely to occur when the client is taught and learns something in the course of his therapy that can be used to enrich his life. Socrates said that the purpose of education should be how to learn how to live well. Each of these direct, straightforward, no-nonsense instructional rebuttals is designed to pique the client's interest in thinking, feeling, and acting differently toward old problems so as to live better. Each response provided can result in branching off into newer and bolder problem-solving suggestions. If psychotherapy that is worth its salt goes beyond:

- Insight;
- Simple reassurance;
- Authoritarian prescriptions for solutions without presenting education for better control of human thoughts and feelings;
- Unreflective abreactive expressions of unwanted emotions whereby the expresser temporarily *feels* better but because he doesn't confront the issue of how he is upsetting himself, misses the demanding jugular vein of emotional disturbance, and as a consequence *gets* worse;
- Paradoxical cleverness and trickery;
- Controlling for success so as to make oneself into an alleged "better" or more "esteemed" person;
- Weeding out a symptom by reshaping or strategically realigning the clients' systems;
- and instead of any or all of the above forthrightly, directly, and unashamedly it teaches something by way of emotional reeducation;

then the tact and tactics identified, inventoried, and illustrated as they echo from from both sides of the desk are likewise worth their salt.

Index